NORTHERN ITALY TRAVEL GUIDE 2025

Explore Charming Streets, Crystal-Clear Lakes, and Historic Cities off the Beaten Path

BY

RUSSELL E. JONES

ALL RIGHTS RESERVED.

No part of this publication may be reproduced, distributed, or transmitted in any form or by any means, including photocopying, recording, or other electronic or mechanical methods, without the prior written permission of the publisher, except in the case of brief quotations embodied in critical reviews and certain other noncommercial uses permitted by copyright law.

DISCLAIMER

This travel guide is provided for informational purposes only. The information contained herein is believed to be accurate and reliable as of the publication date, but may be subject to change. We are not making any warranty, express or implied, with respect to the content of this guide.

Users of this guide are responsible for verifying information independently and consulting appropriate authorities and resources prior to travel. We are not liable for any loss or damage caused by the reliance on information contained in this guide.

Information regarding travel advisories, visas, health, safety, and other important considerations can change rapidly. Users are advised to check for the most up-to-date information from official government and travel industry sources before embarking on any trip.

Travel inherently involves risk, and users are responsible for making their own informed decisions and accepting any associated risks.

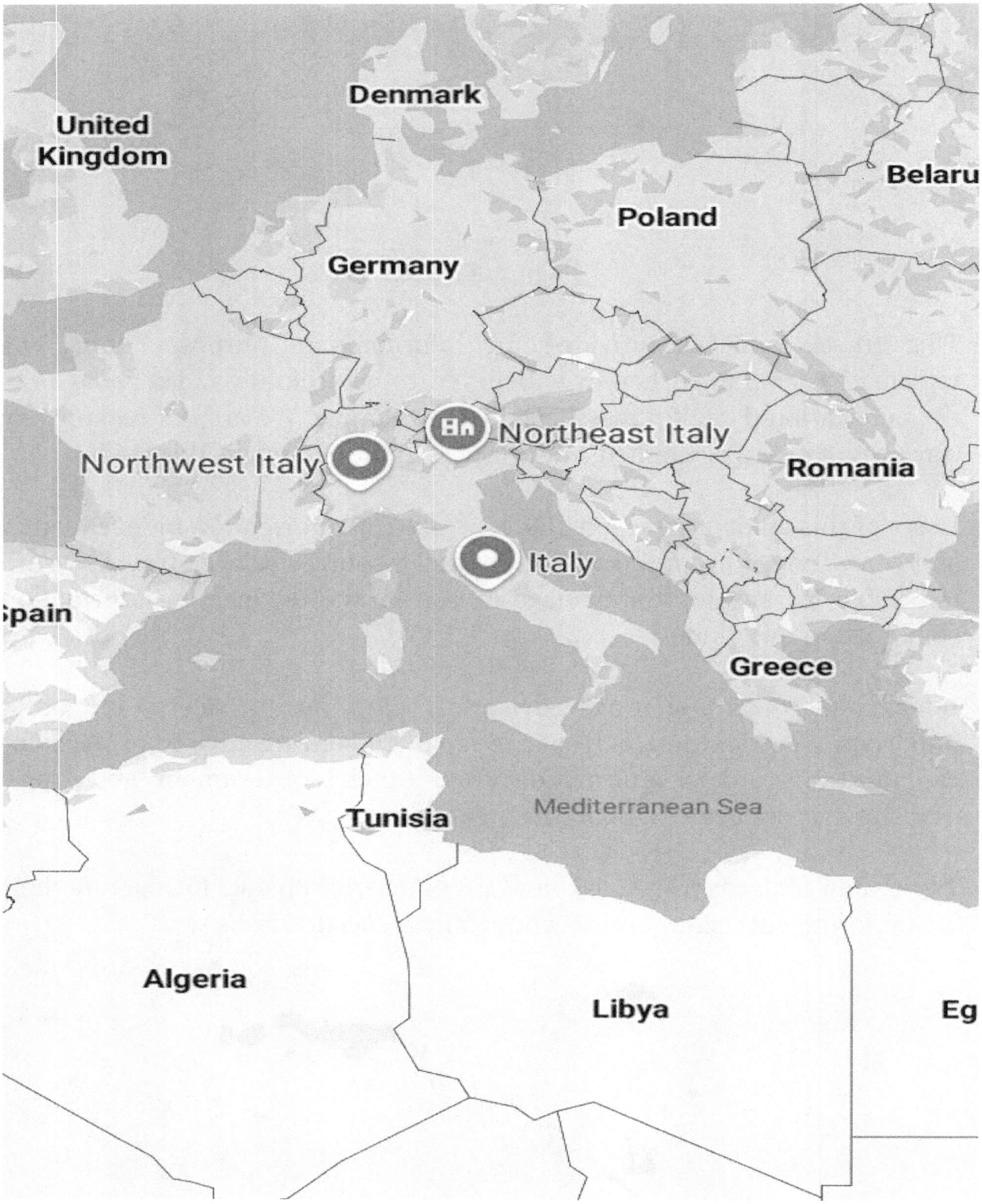
Denmark
United Kingdom
Belaru
Poland
Germany
Northeast Italy
Northwest Italy
Romania
Italy
Spain
Greece
Tunisia
Mediterranean Sea
Algeria
Libya
Eg

TABLE OF CONTENT

Chapter 1. Introduction..6
    1.1 Why Visit Northern Italy in 2025...6
    1.2 Overview of Northern Italy's Regions...8
    1.3 Essential Travel Information..10
    1.4 Best Times to Visit...12

Chapter 2. Planning Your Trip..15
    2.1 Travel Requirements and Documentation...15
    2.2 Getting to Northern Italy...16
    2.3 Transportation Options Within Northern Italy..18
    2.4 Budgeting and Currency Tips..20

Chapter 3. Top Destinations..23
    3.1 Milan – Fashion, Art, and Culture...23
    3.2 Venice – The City of Canals..27
    3.3 Florence – The Renaissance Capital...33
    3.4 Lake Como – Scenic Beauty..38
    3.5 Verona – Romance and Shakespeare..43

Chapter 4. Cultural Experiences..49
    4.1 Italian Cuisine..49
    4.2 Festivals and Events in 2025...50
    4.3 Art and Architecture in Northern Italy...54
    4.4 Language and Local Etiquette in Northern Italy..58

Chapter 5. Outdoor Adventures..63
    5.1 Skiing and Snowboarding in the Dolomites..63
    5.2 Hiking and Mountain Climbing in the Dolomites..66
    5.3 Cycling Trails in Northern Italy..70
    5.4 Exploring the Lakes Region...74

Chapter 6. Regional Highlights..79
    6.1 Lombardy..79
    6.2 Veneto...83
    6.3 Emilia-Romagna...87
    6.4 Trentino-Alto Adige..91

Chapter 7. Accommodations...96
    7.1 Luxury Hotels and Resorts in Northern Italy...96
    7.2 Mid-Range and Boutique Hotels in Northern Italy...100
    7.3 Budget-Friendly Hostels and Guesthouses in Northern Italy........................104
    7.4 Unique Stays – Agriturismos and Historic Villas in Northern Italy...............108

Chapter 8. Food and Drink...113
    8.1 Must-Try Dishes and Local Specialties in Northern Italy.................................. 113
    8.2 Regions of Northern Italy... 116
    8.3 Best Restaurants and Cafes in Northern Italy...119

Chapter 9. Itineraries...124
    9.1 A 7-Day Classic Northern Italy Tour...124
    9.2 A 10-Day Culinary Adventure in Northern Italy..126
    9.3 A 14-Day Comprehensive Road Trip Through Northern Italy........................... 130

Chapter 10. Practical Information...135
    10.1 Currency Exchange and Banking... 135
    10.2 Emergency Services and Health Care..137
    10.3 Safety Tips for Travelers..141

Chapter 11. Sustainable Travel..146
    11.1 Eco-Friendly Travel Tips...146
    11.2 Supporting Local Communities... 150

Chapter 12. Day Trips and Hidden Gems...155
    12.1 Off-the-Beaten-Path Destinations...155
    12.2 Day Trips from Major Cities..159

Chapter 13. Maps and Resources... 163
    13.1 Regional and City Maps...163
    13.2 Useful Travel Apps.. 166
    13.3 Local Contacts and Websites...172

Chapter 14. Final Thoughts and Travel Tips..176
    14.1 Making the Most of Your Trip... 176
    14.2 FAQs for First-Time Visitors..178

Chapter 1. Introduction

1.1 Why Visit Northern Italy in 2025

Northern Italy is a land of timeless beauty, cultural richness, and unforgettable experiences. In 2025, this enchanting region is even more captivating, offering a perfect mix of history, modernity, and unique events that promise to make every traveler's journey memorable. Here's why Northern Italy should be on your travel list this year:

1. A Year of Celebrations and Cultural Events

2025 marks significant anniversaries and new cultural experiences across Northern Italy. Cities like Milan and Venice are hosting internationally renowned art exhibitions, design fairs, and music festivals. Venice's Biennale, known for avant-garde art, promises a spectacular edition, and Milan will showcase fashion weeks that define global trends. These events provide travelers with a front-row seat to Italian creativity and heritage.

2. Iconic Landscapes at Their Best

From the sun-kissed shores of Lake Garda to the dramatic peaks of the Dolomites, Northern Italy boasts some of Europe's most breathtaking scenery. Spring and autumn in 2025 are expected to bring exceptionally vibrant colors due to favorable weather patterns. Winter sports enthusiasts will find pristine conditions in the Italian Alps, with improved infrastructure offering a more seamless experience.

3. Culinary Adventures Like Never Before

Northern Italy's culinary scene in 2025 is flourishing with new Michelin-starred restaurants and innovative dining experiences. Cities like Bologna, Parma, and Modena, famous for rich food traditions, are launching gastronomic tours that combine hands-on cooking classes with immersive tastings. Whether savoring fresh truffle pasta in Piedmont or indulging in risotto alla Milanese, food lovers will find plenty to satisfy their palates.

4. Renaissance Art and Architecture

The cradle of the Renaissance continues to inspire. Florence, Verona, and smaller gems like Mantua and Vicenza offer a blend of ancient wonders and newly restored masterpieces. In 2025, the Uffizi Gallery's enhanced exhibits make navigating its treasures more accessible, and Verona's Arena will host special operatic performances celebrating centuries of musical heritage.

5. Commitment to Sustainable Tourism

Italy is leading a sustainable tourism revolution, and Northern Italy exemplifies this movement. In 2025, expect eco-friendly travel options, including electric ferries in Venice and expanded cycling paths around Lake Como. Many agriturismos now integrate sustainability into their operations, letting visitors enjoy authentic rural stays with minimal environmental impact.

6. Unique Hidden Gems

In 2025, lesser-known destinations like Bergamo (a co-European Capital of Culture), the vineyard landscapes of Langhe-Roero, and the medieval streets of Ferrara offer tranquil escapes from the crowds. New guided tours will help travelers discover charming villages, ancient ruins, and local artisans keeping centuries-old traditions alive.

7. Easy Accessibility and Enhanced Travel Infrastructure

Northern Italy's transportation network is one of the most efficient in Europe. Major investments in rail systems make getting around faster and easier than ever. High-speed trains connect Milan, Venice, Turin, and Florence seamlessly, and regional routes have been upgraded for smoother travel between smaller towns.

In 2025, Northern Italy offers an irresistible combination of history, culture, cuisine, and scenic beauty, all presented in a more accessible, sustainable, and celebratory fashion. Whether you're a first-time visitor or a seasoned traveler, this is the year to immerse yourself in its wonders.

1.2 Overview of Northern Italy's Regions

Northern Italy is a tapestry of diverse regions, each with its unique charm, history, and attractions. From cosmopolitan cities to serene lakeside retreats and alpine adventures, this part of Italy offers an unparalleled variety of experiences. Here's a closer look at the key regions that make Northern Italy an essential destination for travelers:

1. Lombardy (Lombardia)

Capital: Milan
 Why Visit: Lombardy is Italy's economic powerhouse and a hub of fashion, finance, and culture. Milan, its dynamic capital, is famous for landmarks like the Duomo di Milano, La Scala opera house, and the shopping mecca of Galleria Vittorio Emanuele II. Beyond Milan, Lombardy boasts the serene beauty of Lake Como and Lake Garda, perfect for luxury escapes and scenic relaxation. The region also offers UNESCO World Heritage Sites such as the Sacri Monti and the prehistoric rock carvings of Val Camonica.

2. Veneto

Capital: Venice

Why Visit: Veneto's star attraction is Venice, a city of canals, gondolas, and historic splendor. Visitors are captivated by St. Mark's Basilica, the Doge's Palace, and the charm of the Grand Canal. But Veneto offers more than Venice—Verona, the romantic city of *Romeo and Juliet*, and the Prosecco Hills, known for their world-famous sparkling , are must-sees. Padua and Vicenza are rich with art, architecture, and history.

3. Emilia-Romagna

Capital: Bologna

Why Visit: Known as Italy's gastronomic heartland, Emilia-Romagna is home to iconic culinary treasures like Parmigiano-Reggiano cheese, balsamic vinegar of Modena, and prosciutto di Parma. Bologna's medieval streets and porticos make it one of Italy's most picturesque cities, while Ravenna dazzles with Byzantine mosaics. For motorsports enthusiasts, Modena and Maranello offer Ferrari and Lamborghini museums.

4. Piedmont (Piemonte)

Capital: Turin

Why Visit: A land of rolling vineyards, alpine landscapes, and rich history, Piedmont is renowned for its Barolo and Barbaresco s. Turin, a former royal capital, combines grand boulevards and historic cafes with automotive heritage as the birthplace of Fiat. The region is also home to the picturesque Langhe-Roero hills and the charming lakeside town of Stresa on Lake Maggiore.

5. Liguria

Capital: Genoa

Why Visit: Liguria's dramatic coastline is lined with colorful fishing villages, the most famous being the five towns of Cinque Terre. Genoa, with its rich maritime history and stunning palaces, is a hidden gem. Portofino and Santa Margherita Ligure are glamorous seaside retreats, offering crystal-clear waters and delectable seafood.

6. Trentino-Alto Adige

Capital: Trento

Why Visit: This mountainous region offers a fusion of Italian and Austrian culture. The Dolomites, a UNESCO World Heritage Site, are a paradise for outdoor enthusiasts, offering skiing, hiking, and rock climbing. South Tyrol's charming towns, like Bolzano, reflect a unique blend of Tyrolean and Mediterranean influences, with delicious regional cuisine and alpine charm.

7. Friuli Venezia Giulia

Capital: Trieste

Why Visit: Bordering Austria and Slovenia, Friuli Venezia Giulia offers a mix of cultures, languages, and flavors. Trieste's unique Central European character is evident in its architecture and cafes. The region's country produces exceptional whites, and the seaside town of Grado is known for its historic charm and thermal baths.

Each of these regions offers its own allure, from culinary delights and historic landmarks to outdoor adventures and artistic heritage. Exploring Northern Italy is like weaving through a living museum, where every corner reveals a story waiting to be discovered.

1.3 Essential Travel Information

Traveling to Northern Italy in 2025 is an enriching experience filled with stunning landscapes, historic cities, and world-class cuisine. To make your journey smooth and enjoyable, here's a guide to the essential information you'll need to know:

1. Entry Requirements

- **Passports and Visas**: Travelers from the European Union and many other countries (including the United States, Canada, Australia, and the UK) can enter Italy without a visa for stays up to 90 days within a 180-day period.
- **ETIAS Requirement**: Starting in 2025, most non-EU visitors will need an approved ETIAS (European Travel Information and Authorization System) before entering the Schengen Area, including Italy. This electronic authorization is easy to obtain online.
- **Customs**: Check regulations for bringing goods like alcohol, tobacco, and food into Italy to avoid issues at customs.

2. Currency and Payments

- **Currency**: Italy uses the Euro (€).
- **Cash and Cards**: Credit and debit cards are widely accepted in cities and towns, but having cash on hand is useful for small purchases, especially in rural areas and at local markets.
- **ATMs**: Available throughout Northern Italy; look for signs reading *Bancomat*.

3. Language

- **Official Language**: Italian is the primary language spoken. English is commonly spoken in major tourist areas, but learning basic Italian phrases will enhance your experience and help you connect with locals.

4. Transportation

- **Air Travel**: Major international airports in Northern Italy include Milan Malpensa (MXP), Venice Marco Polo (VCE), and Bologna Guglielmo Marconi (BLQ). Regional airports serve smaller cities and provide convenient domestic connections.
- **Trains**: Italy's extensive rail network offers high-speed services connecting major cities (like Milan, Venice, and Florence) and regional trains for smaller towns. Purchase tickets in advance for the best fares on high-speed trains (Trenitalia and Italo).
- **Public Transport**: Buses, trams, and metro systems operate in cities like Milan, Turin, and Bologna. Venice uses vaporettos (water buses) for transportation along its canals.
- **Car Rentals**: Driving is ideal for exploring rural regions, but be aware of limited traffic zones (ZTL) in historic city centers and familiarize yourself with local driving rules.

5. Health and Safety

- **Emergency Numbers**:
    - Medical Emergency: 118
    - Police: 112
    - Fire: 115
- **Health Care**: Italy's public health system is of high quality. Pharmacies (*farmacie*) are well-stocked, and English-speaking doctors can be found in larger cities. Travel insurance is highly recommended to cover medical expenses.
- **Vaccinations**: No special vaccinations are required for entry into Italy, but ensure routine vaccinations are up to date.

6. Climate and Weather

- **Spring (March to May)**: Mild temperatures and blooming flowers, perfect for city explorations and lake visits.
- **Summer (June to August)**: Hot, especially in cities, but ideal for mountain retreats and seaside vacations.
- **Autumn (September to November)**: Cooler, with vibrant foliage and harvest festivals.

- **Winter (December to February)**: Snow in the Alps makes it prime skiing season, while cities are less crowded.

7. Time Zone and Electricity

- **Time Zone**: Central European Time (CET), UTC +1. Daylight Saving Time applies from the last Sunday in March to the last Sunday in October.
- **Electricity**: Italy uses Type F and L plugs, with a standard voltage of 230V. Bring an adapter if your devices use different plug types.

8. Tipping and Etiquette

- **Tipping**: Not obligatory but appreciated. Round up small bills or leave 5-10% at restaurants if service is excellent.
- **Dining Etiquette**: Meals are leisurely experiences. Greet with *Buongiorno* or *Buonasera* and wait for the host to say *Prego* before sitting.

Being prepared with these essentials will help you navigate Northern Italy with confidence, allowing you to fully enjoy its wonders.

1.4 Best Times to Visit

Northern Italy's diverse landscapes, cultural events, and seasonal activities make it a destination worth visiting year-round. However, the best time to explore depends on your interests, preferences, and the experiences you seek. Here's a guide to help you choose the ideal time to visit:

Spring (March to May)

Why Visit in Spring:

- Blooming flowers and lush greenery make spring one of the most picturesque seasons.
- The weather is mild, with average temperatures ranging from 10°C to 20°C (50°F to 68°F), perfect for sightseeing and outdoor adventures.
- Spring is an excellent time to visit the lakes, vineyards, and historic cities before summer crowds arrive.

Highlights:

- Easter celebrations in cities like Florence and Verona, including elaborate processions and traditional events.
- Tulip displays in gardens like Parco Sigurtà near Lake Garda.

- festivals and food fairs celebrating seasonal produce.

Summer (June to August)

Why Visit in Summer:

- Long days and warm weather make summer ideal for lakeside relaxation and mountain excursions.
- Festivals, outdoor concerts, and cultural events are in full swing.
- Coastal regions like Liguria and lakes such as Como and Maggiore are at their most vibrant.

Challenges:

- Temperatures can soar above 30°C (86°F), particularly in cities like Milan and Bologna.
- Popular destinations are crowded, and prices for accommodations peak.

Highlights:

- Venice's Festa del Redentore in July, with spectacular fireworks over the lagoon.
- Outdoor opera performances in Verona's Roman Arena.
- Hiking and cycling in the Dolomites.

Autumn (September to November)

Why Visit in Autumn:

- Cooler temperatures, averaging 10°C to 20°C (50°F to 68°F), create perfect conditions for exploring cities and countryside.
- Vibrant autumn foliage in the Alps and around the lakes adds a magical touch to the landscape.
- Harvest season offers food and festivals that celebrate Italy's culinary heritage.

Highlights:

- The Alba White Truffle Festival in Piedmont, one of Italy's most renowned gourmet events.
- Grape harvest festivals in regions like Veneto and Emilia-Romagna.
- Milan Fashion Week in September, a must for fashion enthusiasts.

Winter (December to February)

Why Visit in Winter:

- Northern Italy's Alps and Dolomites are among Europe's premier ski destinations.
- Cities are less crowded, offering a quieter and more relaxed experience.
- Festive Christmas markets and New Year's celebrations create a magical atmosphere.

Challenges:

- Cold weather, with temperatures often dropping below freezing in the mountains.
- Some rural attractions and smaller towns may have limited services.

Highlights:

- Skiing, snowboarding, and winter sports in resorts like Cortina d'Ampezzo and Bormio.
- Venice's Carnival in February, with its elaborate masks and grand balls.
- Christmas markets in cities like Bolzano and Trento.

Overall Best Times for Different Travelers

- **For Cultural Enthusiasts:** Spring and autumn offer mild weather and fewer crowds.
- **For Outdoor Adventurers:** Summer for lakes and mountains; winter for skiing.
- **For Food and Lovers:** Autumn brings harvest festivals and seasonal specialties.

By understanding Northern Italy's seasons, you can tailor your visit to match your travel style, ensuring a memorable and rewarding experience.

Chapter 2. Planning Your Trip

2.1 Travel Requirements and Documentation

Proper preparation with the right travel documents ensures a smooth journey to Northern Italy. Here's a detailed breakdown of what you'll need to know before your trip in 2025:

1. Passport Requirements

- Your passport must be valid for at least **three months beyond your intended departure date** from the Schengen Area.
- Ensure your passport has at least **two blank pages** for entry and exit stamps.

2. Visa Requirements

- **Short-Stay (Tourist) Visas**:
    - **European Union (EU) and Schengen Area Citizens**: No visa is required.
    - **United States, Canada, Australia, and UK Citizens**: No visa is required for stays up to **90 days within a 180-day period**.
    - **Other Nationalities**: Check Italy's visa requirements specific to your country of citizenship.
- **ETIAS Authorization**:
    - Beginning in 2025, travelers from over 60 countries (including the US, UK, and Australia) must obtain an **ETIAS (European Travel Information and Authorization System)** authorization.
    - **How to Apply**: Applications are submitted online and require a valid passport, a credit or debit card, and an email address. The process typically takes minutes, and approval is generally quick.
    - **Validity**: ETIAS is valid for **multiple entries** over a **three-year period** or until your passport expires.

3. Customs Regulations

- **Duty-Free Allowances**:
    - Tobacco: Up to 200 cigarettes or 100 cigarillos or 50 cigars or 250g of loose tobacco.
- **Prohibited Items**: Weapons, illegal drugs, and certain food items (like meat and dairy from outside the EU) are restricted. Check current rules before travel.

- **Health Insurance**:

- Comprehensive travel insurance is highly recommended to cover medical expenses.
- EU citizens should carry a **European Health Insurance Card (EHIC)** or **Global Health Insurance Card (GHIC)** for access to public health services.

5. Driver's License

- If you plan to drive, an **International Driving Permit (IDP)** is recommended, though not always required for short-term visitors from countries with reciprocal agreements. Check local regulations if renting a car.

By ensuring you have the right travel documents and staying informed about the latest entry requirements, you'll be ready to enjoy a seamless and unforgettable adventure in Northern Italy.

2.2 Getting to Northern Italy

Northern Italy's strategic location and well-developed transport infrastructure make it highly accessible from across Europe and around the world. Whether you prefer flying, taking the train, or driving, here's how to reach the region efficiently and comfortably.

1. By Air

Northern Italy boasts several major international airports:

- **Milan Malpensa Airport (MXP)** – The largest and busiest airport in Northern Italy, offering numerous direct flights from North America, Asia, and Europe.
- **Venice Marco Polo Airport (VCE)** – Ideal for travelers visiting Venice, the Veneto region, and nearby cities.
- **Bologna Guglielmo Marconi Airport (BLQ)** – A key hub for Emilia-Romagna and central Italy.
- **Turin Airport (TRN)** – Convenient for exploring Piedmont and the Italian Alps.
- **Verona Villafranca Airport (VRN)** – Well-positioned for visiting Verona, Lake Garda, and the Dolomites.

Many airlines, including budget carriers, offer direct and connecting flights. For the best fares, book several months in advance and compare multiple airports for flexibility.

2. By Train

Italy's rail network is among the best in Europe, making train travel a popular and efficient option.

- **High-Speed Trains**:

    - **Trenitalia Frecciarossa** and **Italo** trains connect major cities like Milan, Venice, Bologna, and Turin in under 2–3 hours.
    - High-speed trains from Paris, Munich, and Zurich offer direct connections to Milan and Turin.
- **International Connections**:

    - **Thello Trains** (Paris to Milan) and **EuroCity** routes link Switzerland, Austria, and Germany to Northern Italy.
    - For scenic routes, the **Bernina Express** connects Switzerland's Chur to Tirano, offering breathtaking Alpine views.

Tips for Train Travel:

- Book tickets early for the best prices, especially on high-speed routes.
- Validate regional train tickets before boarding to avoid fines.

3. By Car

Driving to Northern Italy is ideal for travelers coming from neighboring countries or exploring rural and less accessible areas.

- **Major Highways (Autostrade)**:
    - **A1 (Autostrada del Sole)**: Links Milan to Florence and Rome.
    - **A4 (Serenissima)**: Connects Turin, Milan, Verona, and Venice.
    - **A22 (Autostrada del Brennero)**: Runs from Austria to Verona via Bolzano.

Toll System:

- Most autostrade are toll roads. Collect a ticket when entering and pay when exiting.
- Payment options include cash, cards, and telepass systems for seamless travel.

Border Crossings:

- Italy shares borders with France, Switzerland, Austria, and Slovenia. Border checks are minimal within the Schengen Area, though random spot checks are possible.

4. By Bus

Long-distance bus services, including **FlixBus** and **Eurolines**, connect major European cities to Northern Italy. Buses are a budget-friendly option but often slower than trains or flights.

5. By Ferry

- **Lake Ferries**: Ferries on **Lake Como, Lake Garda, and Lake Maggiore** are excellent for scenic travel within the region.
- **International Ferries**: Ports like **Venice** and **Trieste** offer routes from Greece, Croatia, and Slovenia.

With so many transportation options available, reaching Northern Italy is simple and customizable to your preferences. Choose the mode of travel that best suits your itinerary, budget, and travel style for an unforgettable journey.

2.3 Transportation Options Within Northern Italy

Navigating Northern Italy is a rewarding experience thanks to its modern transportation network. Whether you're exploring historic cities, scenic lakes, or mountain retreats, multiple options cater to various travel styles. Here's a detailed guide to getting around efficiently and comfortably.

1. Trains

Italy's rail system is extensive, reliable, and often the fastest way to travel between cities.

Key Train Services

- **High-Speed Trains (Alta Velocità)**:
  - **Frecciarossa, Frecciargento, and Frecciabianca (Trenitalia)**: Connect major cities like Milan, Venice, Turin, Bologna, and Verona.
  - **Italo**: A private competitor offering high-speed services on popular routes.
- **Regional Trains**: Connect smaller towns and destinations not served by high-speed lines.

Tips for Train Travel

- Book **high-speed train tickets** in advance for the best prices.
- Regional train tickets must be **validated** before boarding by stamping them at yellow machines on the platform.

- First-class offers more comfort, but second-class is sufficient for most trips.

2. Buses and Coaches

Buses complement the rail network, providing access to rural areas and smaller towns.

City Buses

- Operate extensively in cities like Milan, Turin, Bologna, and Venice. Tickets can be purchased at **tabacchi shops, newsstands**, or metro stations and must be validated upon boarding.
- In Venice, buses are replaced by **vaporettos** (water buses) along the canals.

Intercity Coaches

- Companies like **FlixBus** and **MarinoBus** offer long-distance services at competitive prices, connecting cities not directly linked by train.

3. Metro and Tram Systems

- **Milan**: The most extensive metro network in Northern Italy, with four lines and plans for expansion. Trams and buses offer additional coverage.
- **Turin**: Features a modern metro line complemented by trams and buses.
- **Bologna and Genoa**: Smaller metro and bus systems suitable for city travel.

Tip: Purchase **day passes** or multi-trip tickets for savings if staying in one city for an extended period.

4. Driving and Car Rentals

Renting a car is ideal for exploring the countryside, the Dolomites, or lakeside destinations.

Driving Considerations

- **ZTL Zones (Limited Traffic Zones)**: Most historic city centers restrict vehicle access to residents and permit holders. Violations result in hefty fines.
- **Tolls**: Major highways (autostrade) are toll roads. Payment can be made with cash, cards, or a **Telepass** device.
- **Parking**: Use designated blue spaces (paid parking) and avoid yellow spaces reserved for residents.

Car Rental Requirements

- A valid **driver's license** (an International Driving Permit is recommended for non-EU travelers).
- Minimum age restrictions and additional fees for drivers under 25.

5. Water Transport

- **Venice**: The iconic **vaporetto** system, gondolas, and water taxis navigate the canals.
- **Lakes Como, Garda, and Maggiore**: Ferry services connect charming towns, offering scenic travel options.

6. Bicycles and Scooters

- Many cities have **bike-sharing programs** and scooter rentals, including Milan's **BikeMi** and Turin's **TOBike**.
- In the Dolomites and Lake District, cycling is a popular activity with dedicated bike paths.

7. Taxis and Ride-Sharing

- **Taxis** are metered and available at designated ranks or by phone. Hailing taxis on the street is uncommon.
- **Ride-Sharing**: Apps like **Free Now** and **It Taxi** operate in larger cities, but services like Uber are limited.

By combining these transportation options, travelers can seamlessly explore Northern Italy's cities, countryside, and breathtaking landscapes, making the most of every moment.

2.4 Budgeting and Currency Tips

Planning your budget wisely will enhance your experience in Northern Italy. From dining at trattorias to exploring luxurious destinations, understanding local currency, payment methods, and cost-saving strategies will help you make the most of your trip.

1. Currency and Exchange Rates

- **Currency**: Italy uses the **Euro (€)**.

- **Denominations**: Coins range from 1 cent to 2 euros; banknotes range from 5 to 500 euros.
- **Exchange Rates**: Check rates before departure to estimate your expenses. Currency exchange is available at banks, post offices, and authorized exchange offices. ATMs usually offer better rates than airport kiosks or currency exchange counters.

Tip: Use a credit card with no foreign transaction fees or withdraw cash in larger amounts to minimize ATM fees.

2. Credit and Debit Cards

- **Widely Accepted**: Credit and debit cards (Visa, MasterCard, American Express) are accepted in most urban areas, restaurants, and hotels.
- **Contactless Payments**: Increasingly popular for small purchases. Look for the contactless symbol.
- **PIN Requirement**: Some transactions may require a PIN rather than a signature.

Tip: Notify your bank of your travel plans to avoid potential card blocks for unusual activity.

3. Daily Costs by Budget

Category	Budget Traveler (€)	Mid-Range Traveler (€)	Luxury Traveler (€)
Accommodation	30–80 (hostels, budget hotels)	100–250 (boutique hotels, B&Bs)	300+ (luxury hotels, villas)
Meals	10–20 (street food, casual)	25–50 (trattorias, mid-range)	70+ (fine dining)
Local Transportation	2 (metro/bus)	10–20 (day passes, taxis)	50+ (private transfers)

| Attractions | 10–20 (museums, landmarks) | 30–60 (tours, premium sites) | 100+ (private guides) |

Tip: Look for **combo tickets** or city passes that offer discounts on multiple attractions.

4. Saving Money

- **Accommodation**: Book early and consider staying in smaller towns near major cities for better rates.
- **Food**: Enjoy authentic and affordable meals at **trattorias and osterias** instead of touristy restaurants. Look for places with a "Menu del Giorno" (daily set menu) for good value.
- **Transportation**: Use regional trains instead of high-speed trains for cheaper fares and public transit passes for unlimited travel within cities.
- **Free Attractions**: Many churches, public parks, and historical squares are free to visit. Museums often offer **free admission on the first Sunday of the month**.

5. Tipping Etiquette

- Tipping is **not obligatory** but appreciated for excellent service.
- Restaurants often include a **"coperto" (cover charge)**; round up or leave 5-10% if service exceeds expectations.
- For taxis and other services, rounding up the fare is customary.

By understanding currency use and budgeting practices in Northern Italy, you can plan your expenses efficiently, ensuring you enjoy every moment while keeping costs under control.

Chapter 3. Top Destinations

3.1 Milan – Fashion, Art, and Culture

Milan, the fashion and cultural capital of Italy, seamlessly blends cutting-edge modernity with centuries of rich history. Whether you're drawn to its renowned fashion scene, world-class museums, or iconic landmarks, Milan offers something for every type of traveler. Here's a detailed guide to the top attractions in this vibrant city.

1. The Duomo di Milano (Milan Cathedral)

- **Location**: Piazza del Duomo, Milan, Italy
- **Price**:
    - **Standard Entry**: €5
    - **Cathedrals and Rooftop Entry**: €15–€20
    - **Full Experience (including museum, crypt, and rooftop)**: €20–€25
- **Website**: Duomo di Milano
- **Opening Hours**:
    - **Cathedral**: Daily 8:00 AM – 7:00 PM
    - **Rooftop**: Daily 9:00 AM – 7:00 PM
- **Key Features**:
    - Milan's most iconic landmark, the **Duomo** is one of the largest and most elaborate Gothic cathedrals in the world.
    - Visitors can climb to the rooftop for spectacular panoramic views of Milan and a close-up view of the cathedral's intricate spires and statues.
    - The cathedral also houses important art, including a grand altar and a crypt.

Visitor Services:

- Audio guides and group tours available.
- Gift shop for Milan-themed souvenirs.
- Accessible for visitors with reduced mobility.
- **Tips**: Be aware of dress codes—shoulders and knees must be covered to enter.

Description:
Milan's Duomo di Milano stands as a symbol of the city's grand history and artistic heritage. Its construction began in 1386 and continued for nearly six centuries, making it one of the most impressive architectural feats in the world. The gothic design features 135 spires, 3,400 statues, and stunning stained-glass windows. Visitors can explore the

cathedral's interior, marvel at the art and architecture, and enjoy one of the best views of Milan from the rooftop.

2. The Last Supper by Leonardo da Vinci

- **Location**: Convent of Santa Maria delle Grazie, Via del Monte di Pietà 2, Milan, Italy
- **Price**:
    - **Adults**: €15–€20
    - **Reduced**: €10–€12
- **Website**: The Last Supper Tickets
- **Opening Hours**:
    - Monday–Saturday: 8:15 AM – 7:00 PM
    - Closed on Sundays
- **Key Features**:
    - Leonardo da Vinci's iconic **Last Supper** mural is considered one of the most important works of art in Western history.
    - Painted between 1495 and 1498, the fresco shows the dramatic moment when Jesus announces one of his disciples will betray him.
    - The work is housed in a climate-controlled room to preserve its delicate condition.

Visitor Services:

- Guided tours available.
- Advance reservation required for tickets.
- Audio guides available for a more in-depth understanding of the painting's history and significance.

Description:
Da Vinci's **Last Supper** is perhaps the most renowned piece of Renaissance art, housed in the Convent of Santa Maria delle Grazie in Milan. The mural captures the intense emotional moment when Jesus Christ reveals his impending betrayal, showcasing da Vinci's genius in capturing human emotion and detail. Because of its historical and artistic significance, access is highly restricted, with only a limited number of visitors allowed at a time, making booking tickets well in advance essential.

3. Galleria Vittorio Emanuele II

- **Location**: Piazza del Duomo, Milan, Italy
- **Price**: Free to enter (but shopping and dining options vary in price)
- **Website**: Galleria Vittorio Emanuele II
- **Opening Hours**:
  - Monday–Saturday: 10:00 AM – 7:00 PM
  - Sunday: Closed
- **Key Features**:
  - Milan's famous **shopping arcade**, one of the oldest in the world, is home to luxury boutiques, cafes, and restaurants.
  - The **glass dome** and mosaics on the floor are key highlights, showcasing the stunning architecture.
  - Known for its **fashion heritage**, it's a must-visit for anyone interested in Milan's fashion scene.

Visitor Services:

- Free entry to the gallery itself, but shops and restaurants are open for those looking to indulge in Milan's high-end shopping.
- Guided tours of the architecture are available.
- Wi-Fi and seating available for tourists.

Description:
The **Galleria Vittorio Emanuele II** is Milan's most famous shopping gallery, located between the Duomo and La Scala Opera House. Completed in 1877, this grand, glass-roofed structure features a mix of 19th-century architecture and modern retailing.

It houses some of the world's most prestigious luxury brands, making it a shopping haven for those looking to splurge. Even if you're not shopping, the Galleria is worth visiting for its impressive architecture and cultural significance.

4. Sforza Castle (Castello Sforzesco)

- **Location**: Piazza Castello, Milan, Italy
- **Price**:
  - **Adults**: €10
  - **Reduced**: €5
  - **Free**: On the first Tuesday of the month
- **Website**: Castello Sforzesco
- **Opening Hours**:
  - Daily: 7:00 AM – 7:30 PM (Outdoor areas)
  - Museums: Monday–Friday: 9:00 AM – 5:30 PM, Saturday–Sunday: 9:00 AM – 5:30 PM
- **Key Features**:
  - The **Sforza Castle** is a Renaissance fortress that once housed the powerful Sforza family.
  - Today, it houses several museums and art collections, including works by **Michelangelo**, **Leonardo da Vinci**, and **Raphael**.
  - Visitors can explore its inner courtyards, gardens, and multiple museums.

Visitor Services:

- Audio guides available in multiple languages.
- Restrooms, café, and souvenir shop within the castle.
- Wheelchair access to outdoor areas.

Description:

The **Sforza Castle** is a monumental historical site and a must-see for history and art lovers. Originally built in the 15th century by Francesco Sforza, it played an important role in Milan's political and military history. Today, it is home to several museums, including the Museum of Ancient Art and the Museum of Musical Instruments. Its beautiful grounds and impressive architecture make it a perfect spot for a day of exploration.

5. Pinacoteca di Brera

- **Location**: Via Brera 28, Milan, Italy
- **Price**:
  - **Adults**: €15

- - **Reduced**: €10
  - **Free**: First Sunday of the month
- **Website**: Pinacoteca di Brera
- **Opening Hours**:
  - Tuesday–Sunday: 8:30 AM – 7:15 PM
  - Closed on Mondays
- **Key Features**:
  - A world-class art museum that houses masterpieces by **Caravaggio**, **Raphael**, **Tintoretto**, and other Renaissance artists.
  - A part of the **Brera Art District**, the gallery is renowned for its vast collection of Italian art, ranging from the 14th to the 20th century.

Visitor Services:

- Guided tours and audio guides available.
- Museum café and gift shop.
- Accessibility options for disabled visitors.

Description:
 The **Pinacoteca di Brera** is one of Milan's premier art galleries and a must-visit for art enthusiasts. It is renowned for its collection of Italian Renaissance paintings and its association with the Brera Academy of Fine Arts. The gallery's carefully curated collection features works that span centuries of Italian art history, making it a vital destination for anyone looking to understand Milan's artistic heritage.

Milan is a city that offers much more than just shopping; its historical landmarks, art collections, and cultural treasures make it one of the most well-rounded destinations in Italy. Whether you're interested in fashion, art, or architecture, these attractions provide a deep dive into the heart and soul of Milan.

3.2 Venice – The City of Canals

Venice, often referred to as "The City of Canals," is an enchanting destination that seems frozen in time, with its winding waterways, picturesque bridges, and stunning Renaissance and Gothic architecture. A UNESCO World Heritage Site, Venice offers a unique experience, where every corner is an exploration of beauty and history. Below is a guide to the top attractions in this magical city.

1. St. Mark's Basilica (Basilica di San Marco)

- **Location**: Piazza San Marco, 328, 30124 Venezia VE, Italy
- **Price**:

- - **General Admission**: €5
    - **Special Areas (Treasury, Pala d'Oro)**: €3–€5
    - **Skip-the-Line Tours**: €25–€30
- **Website**: Basilica di San Marco
- **Opening Hours**:
  - **Daily**: 9:30 AM – 5:00 PM
  - **Sunday Mass**: 10:30 AM – 12:00 PM (Free entry during Mass)
- **Key Features**:
  - The **Basilica di San Marco** is one of Venice's most iconic landmarks, known for its intricate mosaics, golden domes, and impressive architecture.
  - The **Pala d'Oro**, an ornate altarpiece encrusted with gold and jewels, is one of the main highlights of the church.
  - Visitors can admire the **mosaic-covered interior** and the views over **Piazza San Marco** from the basilica's exterior galleries.

Visitor Services:

- Audio guides and guided tours available in multiple languages.
- Restrooms and a gift shop are located within the basilica.
- Wheelchair access available.

Description:
 St. Mark's Basilica is the heart of Venetian religious life and one of the finest examples of Byzantine architecture. Dating back to the 11th century, it blends Romanesque, Gothic, and Byzantine styles, creating a uniquely Venetian visual experience. The church's gilded mosaics, depicting biblical stories and saints, are one of the highlights, along with the famed **Horses of St. Mark**, four bronze statues that once adorned the exterior. Don't miss a visit to the **Treasury**, where precious relics and ancient artifacts are displayed.

2. Doge's Palace (Palazzo Ducale)

- **Location**: Piazza San Marco, 1, 30124 Venezia VE, Italy
- **Price**:
  - **Adults**: €20
  - **Reduced**: €13
  - **Ticket with Museum Access**: €25
- **Website**: Doge's Palace
- **Opening Hours**:

- **Daily**: 9:00 AM – 7:00 PM
- Closed on December 25 and January 1
- **Key Features**:
  - The **Doge's Palace** is an architectural marvel that was once the residence of Venice's ruling Doges.
  - Visitors can explore the **Grand Council Hall**, **Doge's Apartments**, and the **Bridge of Sighs**, a bridge connecting the palace to the old prisons.
  - The palace is a stunning example of Venetian Gothic architecture, with intricate marble facades and impressive interiors.

Visitor Services:

- Audio guides and guided tours available.
- A café and restaurant located on-site.
- Wheelchair accessible.

Description:
The **Doge's Palace** is one of Venice's most significant landmarks and a must-see for history and architecture lovers. Once home to the Doge, the elected ruler of Venice, the palace is a stunning example of Gothic architecture and Venetian grandeur. With its intricately decorated **Grand Council Hall**, beautiful **Pietra Dura** inlays, and impressive artwork, the palace offers visitors a deep dive into the political and cultural life of Venice during its golden age.

3. Rialto Bridge (Ponte di Rialto)

- **Location**: Sestiere San Polo, 30125 Venezia VE, Italy
- **Price**: Free to visit
- **Website**: Rialto Bridge
- **Opening Hours**: Open 24/7
- **Key Features**:
  - The **Rialto Bridge** is one of the most famous landmarks in Venice and the oldest of the four bridges crossing the Grand Canal.
  - The bridge offers incredible views of the canal and is lined with shops selling Venetian souvenirs, jewelry, and handcrafted goods.
  - The nearby **Rialto Market** is a great place to explore fresh produce and seafood.

Visitor Services:

- The bridge is free to access and can be visited at any time.

- The surrounding **Rialto Market** provides a local shopping experience with fresh food, fish, and produce.
- Plenty of cafés and restaurants nearby for a scenic dining experience.

Description:
The **Rialto Bridge** is an iconic symbol of Venice, connecting the districts of San Marco and San Polo. Built in the late 16th century, it remains one of the most famous and beautiful bridges in the world. The view from the bridge offers a magnificent panorama of the Grand Canal, framed by historic buildings and bustling gondola traffic. The nearby **Rialto Market** is a great place to experience the vibrancy of Venetian commerce and the city's rich culinary traditions.

4. Grand Canal (Canal Grande)

- **Location**: Venice, Italy
- **Price**:
    - **Gondola Ride**: €80–€100 for 30 minutes (standard rate)
    - **Vaporetti (Water Buses)**: €7.50 per trip
- **Website**: Venetian Public Transport
- **Opening Hours**:
    - Open 24/7, with rides operating from early morning until late evening.
- **Key Features**:
    - The **Grand Canal** is the main waterway in Venice, winding through the heart of the city.
    - Lined with opulent palaces, historical buildings, and beautiful churches, the Grand Canal offers a fascinating view into Venice's architectural heritage.
    - **Gondola rides** are a classic way to explore the canal, while **vaporetto** (public water buses) are a more affordable option for transportation.

Visitor Services:

- Gondola rides and vaporetto tickets are available at various piers around the city.
- Many shops and cafes offer views of the Grand Canal.
- Audio guides are available for canal tours.

Description:
The **Grand Canal** is Venice's primary thoroughfare, where the pulse of the city can be felt most vividly. Lined with magnificent palaces and elegant churches, the canal stretches for about 3.8 kilometers (2.4 miles) and is the setting for some of Venice's most stunning views. A **gondola ride** down the canal is a quintessential Venetian experience, offering a unique perspective of the city's historic architecture, while the

vaporetto provides an affordable and practical way to travel the canal from one end to the other.

5. Peggy Guggenheim Collection

- **Location**: Palazzo Venier dei Leoni, Dorsoduro, 30123 Venezia VE, Italy
- **Price**:
    - **Adults**: €15
    - **Reduced**: €10
- **Website**: Peggy Guggenheim Collection
- **Opening Hours**:
    - **Tuesday–Sunday**: 10:00 AM – 6:00 PM
    - Closed on Mondays
- **Key Features**:
    - The **Peggy Guggenheim Collection** houses one of the finest collections of modern art in Europe.
    - The museum includes works by iconic artists such as **Picasso**, **Dali**, **Kandinsky**, and **Pollock**.
    - Located in a beautiful palace on the Grand Canal, the museum also features a garden with sculptures.

Visitor Services:

- Audio guides and private tours available.
- Café and museum shop on-site.
- Wheelchair access.

Description:
The **Peggy Guggenheim Collection** is an essential visit for art lovers. Located in the former home of Peggy Guggenheim, a passionate collector of modern art, this museum houses some of the most important works of the 20th century. Set in a stunning Venetian palazzo on the Grand Canal, the museum's collection spans multiple movements, from surrealism to abstract expressionism, offering visitors a deep dive into the evolution of modern art in Venice.

Venice is a city like no other, where its canals, art, and architecture come together to create a truly unique experience. Whether you're marveling at the intricate mosaics of St. Mark's Basilica, walking through the historical Doge's Palace, or enjoying a gondola ride along the Grand Canal, Venice offers timeless beauty and culture around every corner.

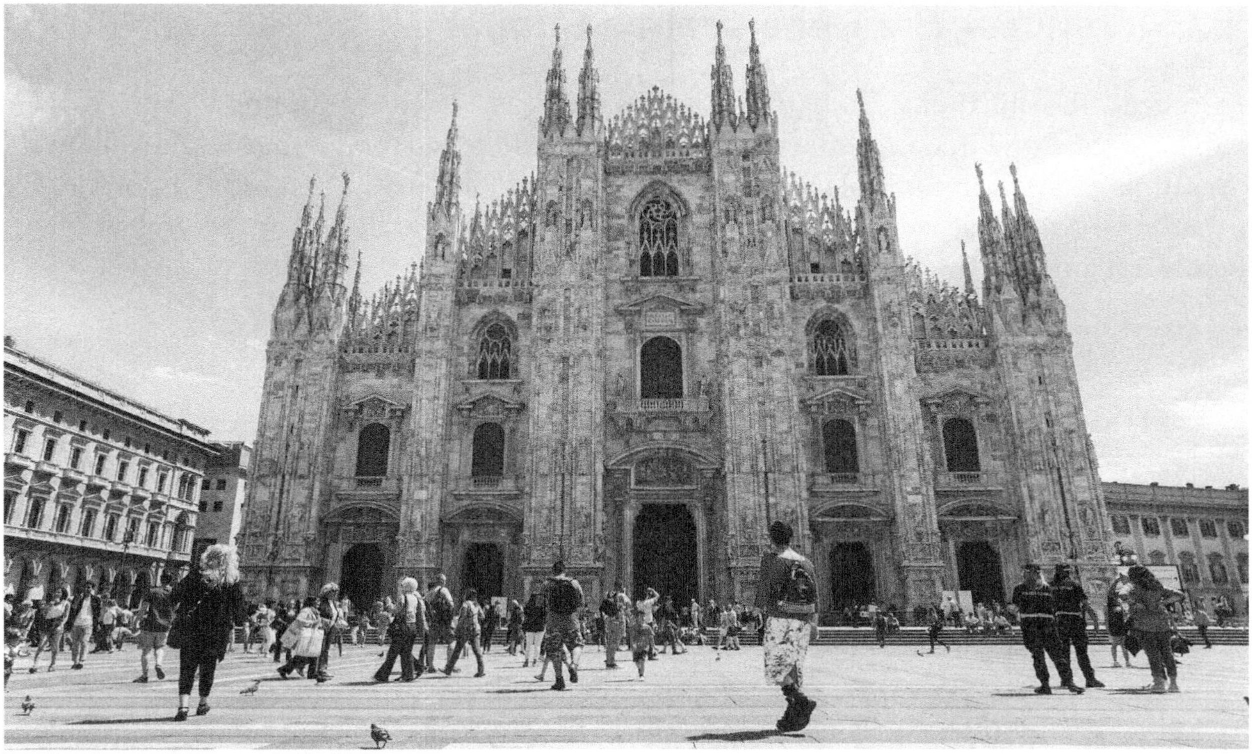

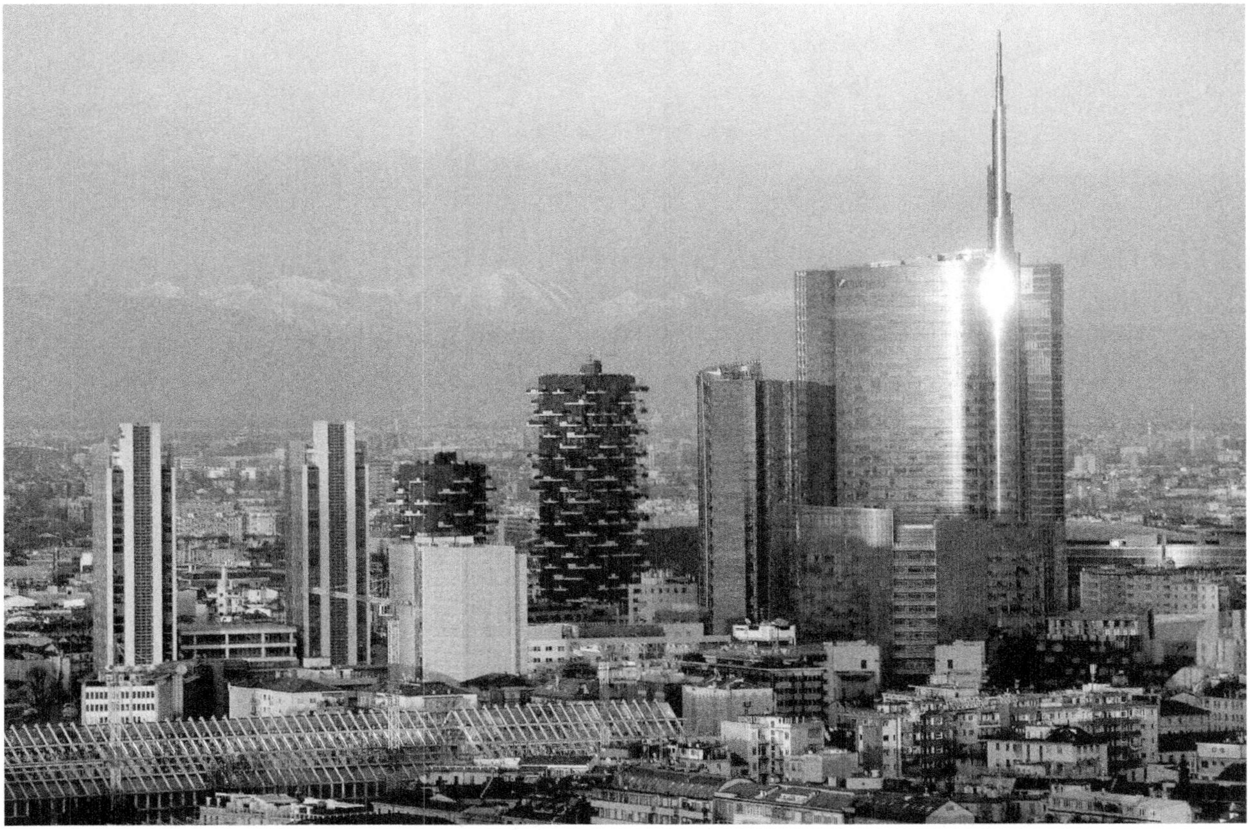

3.3 Florence – The Renaissance Capital

Florence, the birthplace of the Renaissance, is a city brimming with artistic masterpieces, architectural marvels, and centuries-old history. From world-renowned museums to stunning palaces and cathedrals, Florence offers an unforgettable experience for those seeking to immerse themselves in Italy's rich cultural heritage. Below is a guide to the top attractions in this vibrant city.

1. The Uffizi Gallery (Galleria degli Uffizi)

- **Location**: Piazzale degli Uffizi, 6, 50122 Firenze FI, Italy
- **Price**:
    - **Adults**: €20
    - **Reduced**: €10
    - **Ticket with Audioguide**: €25
- **Website**: Uffizi Gallery
- **Opening Hours**:
    - **Tuesday–Sunday**: 8:15 AM – 6:50 PM
    - Closed on Mondays
    - **Closed on 25th December and 1st January**
- **Key Features**:
    - The **Uffizi Gallery** is one of the most famous art museums in the world, housing masterpieces from the **Renaissance**, **Medieval**, and **Baroque** periods.

- Key works include **Botticelli's "The Birth of Venus"**, **Leonardo da Vinci's "Annunciation"**, and **Michelangelo's "Tondo Doni"**.
- The gallery is located in a grand Renaissance building designed by Giorgio Vasari, with spectacular views of the **Arno River** from its windows.

Visitor Services:

- Audioguides and guided tours are available in multiple languages.
- Book tickets in advance, as the gallery often has long lines.
- A café and gift shop are located inside the gallery.
- Wheelchair accessible.

Description:
The **Uffizi Gallery** is a must-visit for art lovers. Housed in the **Uffizi Palace**, originally designed as the offices for Florentine magistrates, the gallery contains one of the richest collections of Italian Renaissance art. Spanning works from the likes of **Caravaggio**, **Raphael**, **Titian**, and **Rembrandt**, it offers an unparalleled opportunity to explore the evolution of Western art. The museum also provides sweeping views of **Piazza della Signoria** and the **Arno River**, making it a visual feast both inside and out.

2. Florence Cathedral (Cattedrale di Santa Maria del Fiore)

- **Location**: Piazza del Duomo, 50122 Firenze FI, Italy
- **Price**:
    - **Cathedral Entry**: Free
    - **Dome Climb**: €20
    - **Dome + Baptistery + Bell Tower Ticket**: €25
- **Website**: Florence Cathedral
- **Opening Hours**:
    - **Cathedral**: Daily, 10:00 AM – 5:00 PM
    - **Dome**: 8:30 AM – 7:00 PM (Closed on the first Sunday of the month)
- **Key Features**:
    - The **Florence Cathedral**, also known as **Santa Maria del Fiore**, is a masterpiece of Gothic architecture.
    - The **brilliant red-tiled dome**, designed by **Filippo Brunelleschi**, dominates the Florence skyline and offers breathtaking views of the city from the top.
    - The **Baptistery of St. John** and **Giotto's Bell Tower** are part of the complex and offer additional insight into the city's medieval architecture and art.

Visitor Services:

- Audioguides and tours available.
- A café and gift shop near the cathedral.
- Wheelchair access to most parts of the cathedral, though the dome is accessible only by climbing.

Description:

The **Florence Cathedral** is the symbol of the city, its majestic dome rising above the Florence skyline as a testament to Renaissance engineering. The cathedral's interior is adorned with stunning frescoes, including **Vasari's Last Judgment** on the dome's interior. Climbing to the top of the dome offers panoramic views of Florence, while the bell tower provides another vantage point over the city. The cathedral complex also includes the **Baptistery**, one of the oldest buildings in Florence, with its celebrated **Gates of Paradise**.

3. Ponte Vecchio

- **Location**: Ponte Vecchio, 50125 Firenze FI, Italy
- **Price**: Free to visit (but shopping may incur costs)
- **Website**: Ponte Vecchio
- **Opening Hours**: Open 24/7
- **Key Features**:
    - The **Ponte Vecchio** is the oldest and most famous bridge in Florence, lined with jewelers, art dealers, and souvenir shops.
    - The bridge's distinctive **goldsmith workshops** and shops make it one of the most picturesque and iconic landmarks in Florence.
    - The **Vasari Corridor**, an elevated passageway built by **Cosimo I de' Medici**, runs above the bridge and connects the **Uffizi Gallery** to the **Pitti Palace**.

Visitor Services:

- The bridge is free to visit, but many of the shops are open for business.
- Perfect for strolling, window shopping, and photography.
- Plenty of cafes along the river for a scenic break.

Description:

The **Ponte Vecchio** is an architectural gem and a symbol of Florence. Built in the 14th century, the bridge has been home to various merchants and craftsmen for centuries. Today, it's a bustling tourist destination, famous for its **goldsmith shops** that date back to the Medici period. The **Vasari Corridor** runs above the bridge and offers an exclusive route through the city, once used by the ruling Medici family to travel privately between the **Uffizi Gallery** and **Pitti Palace**.

4. Palazzo Pitti (Pitti Palace)

- **Location**: Piazza de' Pitti, 1, 50125 Firenze FI, Italy
- **Price**:
    - **Adults**: €16
    - **Reduced**: €10
    - **Full Experience (including museums and gardens)**: €20
- **Website**: Palazzo Pitti
- **Opening Hours**:
    - **Tuesday–Sunday**: 8:15 AM – 6:50 PM
    - Closed on Mondays
- **Key Features**:
    - **Palazzo Pitti** is a Renaissance palace that once housed the powerful **Medici family**.
    - It now houses several museums, including the **Palatine Gallery**, which displays works by **Raphael**, **Titian**, and **Caravaggio**.
    - The **Boboli Gardens** behind the palace offer a serene escape with sculptures, fountains, and lovely views of Florence.

Visitor Services:

- Audioguides and guided tours available.
- On-site café and restaurant offering Tuscan cuisine.
- Wheelchair access and elevators available.

Description:
Palazzo Pitti is a sprawling Renaissance palace and museum complex that offers visitors a glimpse into the grandeur of the Medici dynasty. Built by the **Pitti family**, the palace was later acquired by the Medici and became their primary residence. Today, the palace houses several galleries with stunning works of art, while the **Boboli Gardens** provide an idyllic space for relaxation, with beautiful fountains, sculptures, and panoramic views of Florence.

5. Accademia Gallery (Galleria dell'Accademia)

- **Location**: Via Ricasoli, 58/60, 50122 Firenze FI, Italy
- **Price**:
    - **Adults**: €12
    - **Reduced**: €6

- **Website**: Accademia Gallery
- **Opening Hours**:
  - **Monday–Sunday**: 8:15 AM – 6:50 PM
  - Closed on the first Monday of each month
- **Key Features**:
  - The **Accademia Gallery** is famous for housing **Michelangelo's "David"**, one of the world's most iconic sculptures.
  - The museum also displays a collection of **Renaissance paintings**, including works by **Giorgio Vasari** and **Francesco Botticini**.

Visitor Services:

- Audio guides and guided tours available.
- Restrooms and a gift shop located within the gallery.
- Wheelchair accessible.

Description:
The **Accademia Gallery** is a must-visit for art lovers, housing a stunning collection of Renaissance masterpieces. The centerpiece is undoubtedly Michelangelo's **"David"**, a marble sculpture that showcases the artist's mastery of human anatomy. Beyond David, the gallery also holds a collection of paintings, sculptures, and frescoes, providing a fascinating look at the evolution of art in Florence during the Renaissance.

Florence, with its unparalleled artistic and architectural heritage, is truly the heart of the Renaissance. From the awe-inspiring **Uffizi Gallery** to the majestic **Florence Cathedral**, the city offers endless opportunities for exploration and immersion into the cultural legacy of Italy. Whether you're an art enthusiast, a history buff, or simply looking to enjoy the city's charming atmosphere, Florence never fails to captivate.

3.4 Lake Como – Scenic Beauty

Lake Como, nestled in the Italian Alps, is a destination of natural beauty and sophistication. Known for its picturesque towns, stunning villas, and crystal-clear waters, this area has long been a favorite retreat for celebrities, artists, and travelers seeking serenity. The combination of majestic mountains, lush greenery, and charming lakeside villages makes Lake Como a must-visit for those looking to experience Italy's most scenic landscapes.

1. Villa del Balbianello

- **Location**: Via Comoedia, 5, 22016 Lenno CO, Italy
- **Price**:
    - **Adults**: €20
    - **Reduced**: €10 (for children and students)
    - **Guided Tour**: €30 (includes entry ticket)
- **Website**: Villa del Balbianello
- **Opening Hours**:
    - **March – November**: 10:00 AM – 6:00 PM
    - **Closed in winter (December to February)**
- **Key Features**:

- A historic villa perched on the shores of Lake Como, **Villa del Balbianello** is renowned for its stunning gardens and breathtaking views of the lake and surrounding mountains.
- The villa is also famous for hosting events and film shoots, including scenes from **James Bond's "Casino Royale"** and **Star Wars: Episode II – Attack of the Clones**.
- The villa is a perfect blend of architecture, nature, and history, with its elegant rooms, terraces, and a spectacular lakeside garden.

Visitor Services:

- Guided tours available in multiple languages.
- A gift shop offering local artisanal products.
- Wheelchair access to the garden, but not to the villa's interior.

Description:
Villa del Balbianello is one of Lake Como's most iconic landmarks, perched on a promontory overlooking the lake with panoramic views. Originally built as a monastery in the 13th century, it was later transformed into a luxurious villa. The villa's gardens are a highlight, with meticulously landscaped terraces leading down to the water's edge. Visitors can explore the elegant interior rooms, which are filled with antiques, art, and historical artifacts. The villa is also a popular spot for private events and weddings, offering an enchanting backdrop for special occasions.

2. Villa Carlotta

- **Location**: Via Regina, 2, 22016 Tremezzo CO, Italy
- **Price**:
    - **Adults**: €10
    - **Reduced**: €5 (children 4–12 years)
    - **Seasonal Pass**: €18 (for multiple visits during the year)
- **Website**: Villa Carlotta
- **Opening Hours**:
    - **April – October**: 9:00 AM – 7:00 PM
    - **November – March**: 10:00 AM – 5:00 PM
- **Key Features**:
    - **Villa Carlotta** is a stunning example of Italian neoclassical architecture, set amidst beautiful **botanical gardens**.
    - The villa is home to a renowned collection of art, including works by **Antonio Canova** and **Francesco Hayez**.
    - The gardens are famous for their **magnificent azaleas**, **rhododendrons**, and panoramic views of the lake.

Visitor Services:

- Guided tours available in multiple languages.
- The villa offers a café and restaurant with lakeside views.
- A gift shop specializing in art books and local crafts.
- Wheelchair accessible to the gardens, but limited access to the villa's interior.

Description:

Villa Carlotta is a beautiful historical villa and botanical garden located on the western shore of Lake Como. The villa's neoclassical design and the collection of 19th-century sculptures inside are complemented by the stunning surrounding gardens, which boast over 150 species of plants, including rare and exotic flowers. The gardens are particularly spectacular in spring when the azaleas and rhododendrons bloom. Villa Carlotta is a peaceful retreat offering spectacular views of the lake and the surrounding mountains, and it's a perfect place for art lovers and nature enthusiasts alike.

3. Bellagio – The Pearl of Lake Como

- **Location**: Bellagio, 22021 CO, Italy
- **Price**: Free to visit, but guided tours and boat rides available starting at €10
- **Website**: Bellagio Tourism
- **Opening Hours**: Open year-round, although some shops and attractions may close in winter
- **Key Features**:
    - Bellagio is often called the "Pearl of Lake Como" for its breathtaking position at the intersection of the lake's three branches.
    - The town offers charming cobblestone streets, historic villas, stunning gardens, and panoramic views.
    - Notable sites include **Villa Melzi**, **Punta Spartivento**, and the picturesque **Lungolago** promenade.

Visitor Services:

- Boat tours and private yacht rentals are available to explore the lake.
- Bellagio offers numerous lakeside cafes, restaurants, and shops, perfect for a leisurely afternoon.
- Free Wi-Fi in some public spaces.

Description:

Bellagio is one of the most picturesque towns on Lake Como, nestled on a promontory between the lake's three arms. The town is known for its beautiful cobblestone streets, colorful houses, and sophisticated atmosphere. Visitors can stroll along the **Lungolago**, enjoy breathtaking views of the lake, or relax in the lush gardens of **Villa Melzi**. For those interested in history, **Punta Spartivento** provides a lovely vantage point of the town's historic and scenic beauty. Bellagio is also a great starting point for boat trips across the lake, with ferry services linking the town to other famous lakeside villages.

4. Como Town

- **Location**: Como, 22100 CO, Italy
- **Price**:
  - **Como Cathedral Entry**: Free
  - **Funicular to Brunate**: €5.50 (one way)
- **Website**: Como Tourism
- **Opening Hours**:
  - **Como Cathedral**: Daily, 9:00 AM – 7:00 PM
  - **Funicular**: 8:00 AM – 8:00 PM
- **Key Features**:
  - **Como Cathedral (Cattedrale di Santa Maria Assunta)** is an architectural gem in the heart of Como, featuring a blend of Gothic and Renaissance styles.
  - **Funicular ride to Brunate** offers panoramic views of the lake and the surrounding Alps.
  - The **Piazza Cavour** and **Lungolago** promenade provide scenic spaces for relaxation, shopping, and dining.

Visitor Services:

- Visitor centers around Como provide maps and information about local attractions.
- Restaurants, cafes, and shops are plentiful in the town center.
- Free Wi-Fi in some public areas.

Description:
The town of **Como** is the main gateway to Lake Como, with its historic **cathedral**, charming town square, and scenic lakeside promenade. The **Como Cathedral** features intricate sculptures and beautiful stained glass windows, showcasing the city's artistic heritage. A highlight of Como is the **Funicular** ride to **Brunate**, a hilltop village that offers panoramic views of the town and lake. Como's central **Piazza Cavour** is perfect for a leisurely stroll, surrounded by cafes, boutiques, and historic buildings. From here, visitors can easily access ferries to other towns around the lake.

5. Isola Comacina

- **Location**: Near Ossuccio, Lake Como, Italy
- **Price**:
  - **Boat Ride to the Island**: €10–€15 (round trip)
  - **Restaurant Meal on the Island**: Prices vary, typically €25–€50 per person
- **Website**: [Isola Comacina](#)
- **Opening Hours**: Accessible by boat (no set hours, but best to visit in daylight)
- **Key Features**:
  - **Isola Comacina** is the only island on Lake Como and is known for its ancient ruins, rich history, and beautiful natural surroundings.
  - The island is home to the **San Giovanni Church** and offers hiking trails with spectacular views.
  - The island is famous for its annual **Festival of San Giovanni** and for its charming restaurants serving local cuisine.

Visitor Services:

- Boat rides to the island available from the nearby towns of **Ossuccio** and **Lenno**.
- Restaurants on the island offer traditional Italian and Lombard cuisine, especially **lake fish**.

Description:

Isola Comacina is a serene and historical island located in the western part of Lake Como. The island has been inhabited since Roman times, and its remnants include **ancient churches**, medieval ruins, and picturesque gardens. Visitors can explore the **San Giovanni Church** and take in the peaceful atmosphere as they wander the island's quiet paths. For those looking for a memorable dining

experience, the island is known for its delicious local dishes, with several restaurants offering views of the lake.

Lake Como offers a variety of activities and attractions, from exploring historic villas to relaxing in the charming lakeside towns. Whether you're an avid history lover, nature enthusiast, or simply seeking a beautiful and tranquil getaway, Lake Como provides the perfect setting. Its combination of historical landmarks, serene landscapes, and cultural attractions makes it a unique destination worth visiting.

3.5 Verona – Romance and Shakespeare

Verona, a city of history, art, and romance, is forever immortalized by Shakespeare's tragic love story of **Romeo and Juliet**. Located in the Veneto region of Northern Italy, Verona is not just a destination for literature lovers but also a place rich in Roman and medieval history. With its beautiful architecture, charming streets, and vibrant cultural scene, Verona is an enchanting city that captivates visitors year-round.

1. Juliet's House (Casa di Giulietta)

- **Location**: Via Cappello, 23, 37121 Verona VR, Italy
- **Price**:
    - **Adults**: €6
    - **Reduced**: €4 (students, children 6–18 years)
    - **Under 6**: Free
- **Website**: Casa di Giulietta
- **Opening Hours**:
    - **Monday – Sunday**: 8:30 AM – 7:30 PM
- **Key Features**:
    - **Juliet's House** is one of the most iconic landmarks in Verona.

- The house features a **balcony** that is famously associated with Shakespeare's play, and the **statue of Juliet** is a popular photo opportunity.
- Inside, visitors can explore a small museum dedicated to the history of the house, Shakespeare's play, and the legendary love story.

Visitor Services:

- Audio guides available in multiple languages.
- Souvenir shop selling items related to Juliet and Shakespeare.
- **Juliet's Wall** outside the house is covered with love notes from visitors around the world.

Description:
Juliet's House is the focal point of Verona's association with Shakespeare's play. The house itself is a beautiful example of medieval architecture, and the **balcony** has become a symbol of eternal love. Visitors can stand in the courtyard and imagine the famous balcony scene, as well as leave their own love notes on the walls. Inside the house, a museum exhibits letters, writings, and artifacts that explore the history of Juliet, both as a literary figure and as part of Verona's folklore. The atmosphere around the house is filled with romantic energy, making it a must-see for fans of the play and lovers of history alike.

2. Verona Arena (Arena di Verona)

- **Location**: Piazza Bra, 1, 37121 Verona VR, Italy
- **Price**:
  - **Adults**: €10
  - **Reduced**: €4 (students, children 6–12 years)
  - **Under 6**: Free
- **Website**: Arena di Verona
- **Opening Hours**:
  - **April – October**: 9:00 AM – 7:30 PM
  - **November – March**: 10:00 AM – 5:00 PM
- **Key Features**:
  - The **Verona Arena** is one of the best-preserved ancient Roman amphitheaters in the world.
  - It is still used today for large-scale performances, particularly the **Arena di Verona Opera Festival**.
  - Visitors can explore the **arena's inner chambers** and stand in the seats where thousands of spectators once watched gladiatorial combat.

Visitor Services:

- Guided tours available in multiple languages.
- Access to an exhibition showcasing the history of the Arena and its famous events.
- The Arena hosts a variety of events, including operas, concerts, and other performances.

Description:
The **Verona Arena** is a spectacular Roman amphitheater built in the 1st century AD and has a capacity of up to 15,000 spectators. Unlike many ancient sites, the Arena is still used today for concerts and operas, making it a living testament to the enduring legacy of Roman architecture and entertainment. Visitors can admire the arena's impressive structure, explore its ancient passages, and experience the ambiance of an ancient performance venue. The **Arena di Verona Opera Festival**, held every summer, is a world-renowned event, drawing opera lovers from around the globe to experience timeless performances in this stunning historical setting.

3. Piazza delle Erbe

- **Location**: Piazza delle Erbe, 37121 Verona VR, Italy
- **Price**: Free
- **Website**: Piazza delle Erbe

- **Opening Hours**: Open year-round, although some shops and markets may close in winter.
- **Key Features**:
  - The **Piazza delle Erbe** is the heart of Verona's historic center, surrounded by medieval buildings, frescoed palaces, and elegant fountains.
  - The **Torre dei Lamberti** stands tall in the square, offering panoramic views of the city.
  - The square also hosts a **daily market**, where visitors can buy fresh produce, local goods, and unique souvenirs.

Visitor Services:

- The square is surrounded by cafes and restaurants, perfect for a break while exploring the city.
- Information booths are available for tourists to get maps and event details.
- Accessible to all, with wheelchair access.

Description:
The **Piazza delle Erbe** is one of the most picturesque squares in Verona. Dating back to Roman times, it has always been a center for commerce and social life. Today, the square is a bustling hub, with local vendors, cafes, and tourists mingling in its vibrant atmosphere. Dominating the square is the **Torre dei Lamberti**, a 84-meter-high tower that provides visitors with a stunning view of Verona. The square is also home to several important historical buildings, including the **Palazzo Maffei**, and is a perfect spot to relax while soaking in the charm of the city.

4. Castelvecchio and Ponte Scaligero

- **Location**: Corso Castelvecchio, 2, 37121 Verona VR, Italy
- **Price**:
  - **Adults**: €6
  - **Reduced**: €4 (students, children 6–12 years)
- **Website**: Castelvecchio Museum
- **Opening Hours**:
  - **Tuesday – Sunday**: 8:30 AM – 7:30 PM
  - **Closed on Mondays**
- **Key Features**:
  - **Castelvecchio** is a medieval fortress that once served as the seat of the Scaligeri family, rulers of Verona.
  - The **Ponte Scaligero**, the bridge connecting the castle to the city, is an engineering marvel, offering scenic views over the Adige River.

- Inside the castle, visitors will find the **Castelvecchio Museum**, which houses a collection of medieval art, sculptures, and weapons.

Visitor Services:

- Audio guides available.
- The museum includes a gift shop featuring local artwork and souvenirs.
- There is a café on the castle grounds, offering a relaxing space with views of the river.

Description:
Castelvecchio is a magnificent fortress dating back to the 14th century, originally built to defend the Scaligeri family. Today, it houses the **Castelvecchio Museum**, a museum showcasing Verona's medieval art, sculpture, and history. The **Ponte Scaligero**, the bridge leading out from the castle, is one of Verona's most photographed landmarks, offering breathtaking views of the river and surrounding landscape. The castle and bridge stand as testaments to Verona's medieval military might, and visiting them gives a fascinating insight into the city's rich history.

5. Verona Cathedral (Cattedrale di Santa Maria Matricolare)

- **Location**: Piazza Duomo, 37121 Verona VR, Italy
- **Price**:
  - **Adults**: €5
  - **Reduced**: €3 (students, children 6–12 years)
- **Website**: Verona Cathedral
- **Opening Hours**:
  - **Monday – Saturday**: 9:00 AM – 6:00 PM
  - **Sunday**: 9:00 AM – 12:00 PM, 4:00 PM – 6:00 PM
- **Key Features**:
  - The **Verona Cathedral** is a stunning example of Romanesque and Gothic architecture, with a striking façade and intricate frescoes.
  - Inside the cathedral, visitors will find beautiful **Renaissance art** and ornate chapels.
  - The **Basilica of San Zeno**, another church in Verona, is also worth visiting for its impressive architecture and historical significance.

Visitor Services:

- Guided tours available for groups and individual visitors.
- There is a small café and gift shop within the cathedral.
- The cathedral is easily accessible from the city center.

Description:
The **Verona Cathedral**, dedicated to **Santa Maria Matricolare**, is a breathtaking example of Verona's religious and artistic heritage. The cathedral's façade is a beautiful blend of Romanesque and Gothic styles, and inside, the serene atmosphere and artistic works make it an unforgettable stop on a Verona tour. The cathedral is famous for its **Renaissance altarpiece** and frescoed vaults. It is a place of both spiritual and cultural importance, offering visitors a chance to admire both art and architecture in one of Verona's oldest buildings.

Verona is a city steeped in history, art, and romance. From the iconic **Juliet's House** to the grand **Verona Arena**, every corner of the city tells a story. The charming squares, historic buildings, and beautiful churches make Verona a captivating destination for history lovers, Shakespeare enthusiasts, and those looking to experience the romantic allure of Italy. Whether you're exploring its medieval castles, strolling its romantic streets, or enjoying the vibrant local culture, Verona offers something for everyone.

Chapter 4. Cultural Experiences

4.1 Italian Cuisine

Italy is globally renowned for its culinary traditions, and Northern Italy, in particular, boasts a rich variety of regional dishes, ingredients, and s. The cuisine of Northern Italy is characterized by its use of fresh, local ingredients, often with a focus on risottos, polenta, fresh seafood, and hearty meat dishes, all complemented by a world-class selection. This section explores the diverse flavors and culinary experiences you can enjoy in Northern Italy, providing an in-depth look at regional specialties and pairings.

1. Regional Cuisine in Northern Italy

The culinary landscape of Northern Italy differs greatly from that of the south, with a stronger emphasis on rice, butter, and cream, as opposed to pasta and olive oil. Below are some of the key dishes and culinary influences from the region:

1.1 Risotto – A Northern Italian Staple

- **Key Dishes**:
    - **Risotto alla Milanese**: This iconic dish from Milan features rice cooked with saffron and a generous helping of butter and Parmesan cheese, giving it a rich and golden color.
    - **Risotto al Nero di Seppia**: A Venetian specialty, this risotto is flavored with cuttlefish ink, creating a striking black color and a deep, oceanic taste.
    - **Risotto al Barolo**: Hailing from the Piedmont region, this risotto is made with Barolo , giving it a complex, earthy flavor.

1.2 Polenta – Comfort Food of the North

- **Key Dishes**:
    - **Polenta Taragna**: A dish from the Lombardy and Piedmont regions, this polenta is made with cornmeal and buckwheat flour, often served with melted cheese, butter, and meats like sausages or braised beef.
    - **Polenta con Salsiccia**: A traditional dish where polenta is served with a variety of sausages and rich sauces.

1.3 Hearty Meats and Stews

- **Key Dishes**:
  - **Osso Buco**: A classic Milanese dish made from braised veal shanks, served with gremolata, a tangy topping made with lemon zest, garlic, and parsley.
  - **Brasato al Barolo**: A braised beef dish from Piedmont, slow-cooked in Barolo , resulting in a tender and flavorful meal.
  - **Spezzatino**: A rich meat stew, typically made with beef, pork, or lamb, and flavored with local herbs and vegetables.

1.4 Freshwater Fish and Seafood

Northern Italy is home to several lakes, which contribute to a vibrant seafood scene, especially in regions like **Lombardy** and **Veneto**. Some notable fish dishes include:

- **Pesce di Lago**: Freshwater fish like perch, trout, and pike, which are commonly served grilled, baked, or in a savory stew.
- **Risotto ai Frutti di Mare**: A seafood risotto made with a combination of shellfish, mollusks, and sometimes freshwater fish, commonly found in regions like **Veneto** and **Friuli Venezia Giulia**.

4.2 Festivals and Events in 2025

Northern Italy is home to a rich cultural heritage, and throughout 2025, the region will host a variety of festivals and events that celebrate its history, art, music, food, and traditions. From grand international events to local celebrations, these festivals offer an incredible opportunity to immerse yourself in Italian culture and experience the unique charm of Northern Italy.

1. Milan Fashion Week – February and September 2025

- **Location**: Milan, Lombardy
- **Date**:
  - **Women's Fashion Week**: February 18 – 24, 2025
  - **Men's Fashion Week**: September 2025 (Exact dates TBA)
- **Key Features**:
  - Milan is one of the fashion capitals of the world, and the Fashion Week is a major event in the global fashion calendar.
  - Featuring runway shows, presentations, and pop-up events from top designers and emerging talents.
  - Attended by celebrities, influencers, buyers, and fashion enthusiasts.
- **Visitor Services**:

- Access to fashion shows often requires invitations, but various events such as showroom exhibitions and fashion-related exhibitions are open to the public.
- Guided city tours and shopping experiences are available for fashion lovers who want to explore Milan's fashion scene.
- **Description**:

   Milan Fashion Week is one of the most prestigious events in the fashion world, attracting designers, models, and fashion lovers from all over the globe. In 2025, the city will again showcase its haute couture, luxury brands, and avant-garde designs. Beyond the runway shows, the city itself will become a hub of fashion-related activities, including art exhibitions, exclusive parties, and pop-up events. For those interested in fashion, this event is an absolute must.

2. Venice Carnival – February 2025

- **Location**: Venice, Veneto
- **Date**: February 7 – 25, 2025
- **Key Features**:
  - Famous for its elaborate masks and costumes.
  - Public processions, masquerade balls, music performances, and traditional Venetian events.
  - The **Flight of the Angel** on the first day of the Carnival and the **Best Mask Contest**.
- **Visitor Services**:
  - Mask-making workshops.
  - Traditional Venetian sweets and treats, including **frittelle** (fried dough pastries) and **galani** (crispy cookies).
  - Canal boat tours and gondola rides with a festive touch during the Carnival.
- **Description**:

   The **Venice Carnival** is one of the most iconic celebrations in Italy, attracting thousands of visitors from around the world. The streets and canals of Venice come alive with color, as participants don elaborate costumes and masks, evoking the city's historic grandeur. Parades and performances take place throughout the festival, with a particular highlight being the traditional **Flight of the Angel**, where a young woman descends from the Campanile (bell tower) in a grand spectacle. The Carnival's rich history dates back to the 12th century, and it remains a captivating display of Venetian culture and artistic expression.

3. Verona Opera Festival – June to August 2025

- **Location**: Verona Arena, Verona, Veneto

- **Date**: June 13 – August 30, 2025
- **Key Features**:
  - An open-air opera festival held in the **Verona Arena**, one of the largest and best-preserved Roman amphitheaters.
  - World-class opera performances, including works by **Verdi**, **Puccini**, and **Verismo composers**.
  - Performances under the stars with spectacular staging and acoustics.
- **Visitor Services**:
  - Guided tours of the Verona Arena.
  - Exclusive opera packages that include tickets to performances, behind-the-scenes access, and accommodation options.
  - Opera-related workshops for those interested in learning more about the art form.
- **Description**:

 Verona's **Arena** hosts one of the most celebrated opera festivals in the world, and 2025 promises an exciting lineup. Set in a 2,000-year-old Roman amphitheater, the festival showcases spectacular performances by some of the world's top opera singers. The open-air setting adds to the grandeur of the experience, with the natural acoustics of the Arena amplifying the power of the performances. The **Verona Opera Festival** is an extraordinary event for music lovers and cultural enthusiasts, offering an unforgettable way to experience Italy's operatic heritage.

4. Trentino Music Festival – July 2025

- **Location**: Various locations in Trentino, Trentino-Alto Adige
- **Date**: July 1 – 31, 2025
- **Key Features**:
  - Classical music performances held in some of the most scenic venues of the Trentino region, including historic churches, castles, and outdoor amphitheaters.
  - A mix of symphonic, chamber, and choral music, with performances by world-renowned musicians.
  - Celebrates the region's rich musical tradition, with performances by local and international artists.
- **Visitor Services**:
  - Concert tickets available for individual performances or full festival passes.
  - Guided tours of the historic venues hosting the concerts, such as **Castel Thun** and **Palazzo Roccabruna**.
  - Local cuisine and pairings available at concert venues, with a chance to enjoy the regional specialties.

- **Description**:
  The **Trentino Music Festival** brings together the beauty of the Dolomites and the timeless elegance of classical music. Held throughout the picturesque region of **Trentino**, the festival offers an array of performances in stunning historical settings. Visitors can enjoy a mix of solo recitals, symphonic orchestras, and opera performances. This festival is a treat for both music lovers and those who appreciate the stunning natural landscapes of Northern Italy.

5. Festa della Madonna Bruna – July 2, 2025

- **Location**: **Alessandria**, Piedmont
- **Date**: July 2, 2025
- **Key Features**:
  - A traditional festival honoring the **Madonna Bruna**, the patron saint of Alessandria.
  - A colorful procession featuring a life-sized statue of the Madonna carried through the city by local participants.
  - Music, fireworks, and local street food are an integral part of the celebrations.
- **Visitor Services**:
  - Local guided walking tours that offer historical context about the festival and its significance.
  - Street food stalls offering traditional delicacies such as **focaccia**, **grissini**, and **bagna càuda** (a warm garlic and anchovy dip).
- **Description**:
  The **Festa della Madonna Bruna** in **Alessandria** is one of the region's most important religious celebrations. The festival dates back to the 17th century and is characterized by a stunning procession that winds its way through the city's streets. The main highlight is the **Madonna's statue**, which is carried on a grand float through the crowds, while music and fireworks light up the night sky. It is a perfect blend of religious reverence and festive enjoyment, offering a deep dive into local traditions and culture.

6. The International Truffle Fair – November 2025

- **Location**: **Alba**, Piedmont
- **Date**: October 6 – November 15, 2025
- **Key Features**:
  - A celebration of **white truffles**, one of the most sought-after delicacies in Italy.
  - Truffle markets, tastings, cooking demonstrations, and chef-led truffle hunts.

- - Truffle auctions where rare and prized truffles are sold.
- **Visitor Services**:
  - Truffle hunting experiences with expert guides and trained dogs.
  - Cooking classes focusing on how to incorporate truffles into gourmet dishes.
  - Truffle-themed and food pairing dinners at local restaurants.
- **Description**:
  The **International Truffle Fair** in **Alba** is the highlight of the truffle season in Piedmont. Truffles from the surrounding hills are celebrated with a range of events, from auctions and markets to cooking classes and gourmet dinners. It's a unique opportunity for visitors to learn about the prized white truffle, its culinary applications, and its role in Italian gastronomy. Visitors can also join **truffle hunts** led by expert truffle hunters and their specially trained dogs, making it an exciting and educational experience.

Northern Italy's festivals and events in 2025 offer something for everyone—whether you're an art lover, a food enthusiast, or simply looking for a way to celebrate Italy's rich cultural heritage. These events provide a unique opportunity to experience the region's traditions, creativity, and hospitality at their finest. Be sure to mark your calendar for these extraordinary celebrations during your visit!

4.3 Art and Architecture in Northern Italy

Northern Italy is a treasure trove of world-class art and architecture, showcasing centuries of history, innovation, and cultural exchange. From the grandeur of Renaissance palaces and churches to cutting-edge modern architecture, the region offers an incredible variety of artistic and architectural experiences. This section delves into the key elements of Northern Italy's artistic heritage, including must-see museums, landmarks, and artistic movements that shaped the region.

1. The Renaissance – The Heart of Northern Italy's Artistic Legacy

The Renaissance, which began in Florence during the 14th century, spread quickly throughout Northern Italy, influencing art, architecture, and culture for centuries to come. In the cities of Milan, Venice, and Verona, Renaissance masterpieces continue to captivate visitors with their beauty and sophistication.

1.1 Milan – A Hub of Renaissance Art and Architecture

- **Key Attractions**:
  - **The Last Supper by Leonardo da Vinci**: Located in the **Convent of Santa Maria delle Grazie**, Milan, this iconic fresco is one of the most

famous artworks in the world, representing a pinnacle of Renaissance painting.
- **Sforza Castle (Castello Sforzesco)**: A symbol of Milan's Renaissance grandeur, this castle houses several museums, including a museum dedicated to ancient art and the **Pietà Rondanini**, Michelangelo's unfinished sculpture.
- **Milan Cathedral (Duomo di Milano)**: While the Duomo began construction in the Gothic style, its intricate façade and stunning spires reflect a blend of Renaissance and Gothic influences.

1.2 Venice – Renaissance Splendor by the Water

- **Key Attractions**:
  - **Doge's Palace (Palazzo Ducale)**: This Gothic-Renaissance palace is a symbol of Venice's political power, featuring ornate halls, grand staircases, and an incredible view over the Grand Canal.
  - **Basilica di San Marco**: Known for its stunning Byzantine and Renaissance mosaics, this cathedral is one of Venice's architectural gems.
  - **Accademia Gallery**: Home to the most important collection of Venetian Renaissance art, including works by Titian, Bellini, and Veronese.

1.3 Verona – The City of Roman and Renaissance Architecture

- **Key Attractions**:
  - **Piazza delle Erbe**: A vibrant square surrounded by Renaissance and medieval buildings, including the **Torre dei Lamberti**, which offers panoramic views of Verona.
  - **Palazzo della Ragione**: A beautiful example of Venetian Gothic architecture, featuring Renaissance frescoes and a grand medieval hall.
  - **Juliet's House**: Although tied to the Shakespearean play, the house itself is a mix of medieval and Renaissance styles, with a famous balcony.

2. Baroque and Rococo Architecture – Northern Italy's Grandeur

The Baroque period (17th–18th centuries) marked an era of opulence and grandeur, with churches and palaces designed to evoke emotion and awe through dramatic use of space, light, and ornamentation. Cities like Turin and Milan are home to some of the most magnificent Baroque structures in the country.

2.1 Turin – Baroque Elegance

- **Key Attractions**:
  - **The Royal Palace of Turin (Palazzo Reale)**: A stunning example of Baroque architecture, this palace was the seat of the Savoy dynasty and features lavish interiors, including the **Hall of Mirrors** and the **Royal Armoury**.
  - **The Chapel of the Holy Shroud (Capella della Sacra Sindone)**: A Baroque masterpiece designed by Guarino Guarini, this chapel houses the famous Shroud of Turin (currently not on display).
  - **Superga Basilica**: Set on a hilltop, this Baroque basilica offers breathtaking views of the city and is a significant architectural landmark in Turin.

2.2 Milan – Baroque Churches and Monuments

- **Key Attractions**:
  - **Santa Maria della Passione**: A remarkable Baroque church, renowned for its dramatic façade and stunning frescoes by artists like Bernardino Luini.
  - **San Carlo al Corso**: Another exemplary Baroque church in Milan, famous for its grand dome and ornate interior.
  - **The Royal Palace of Milan (Palazzo Reale)**: While the palace's origins date back to the Middle Ages, the Baroque renovation of the structure contributed to its grandeur.

3. Modern and Contemporary Architecture in Northern Italy

While Northern Italy is steeped in centuries of artistic tradition, the region also embraces modern and contemporary architectural movements. Iconic designs from the 20th and 21st centuries showcase Italy's ongoing contributions to architectural innovation.

3.1 Milan – The Epicenter of Modern Design

Milan is the heart of Italy's modern architecture and design scene, constantly evolving while preserving its historical charm.

- **Key Attractions**:
  - **Galleria Vittorio Emanuele II**: A grand shopping gallery that blends 19th-century architecture with innovative design elements, including a glass-and-iron roof that was one of the first of its kind.

- **Fondazione Prada**: A striking example of contemporary architecture, this cultural center in the former gin distillery features bold design elements, including a mix of old and new buildings.
- **CityLife**: A new, cutting-edge district in Milan, home to iconic skyscrapers designed by renowned architects such as Zaha Hadid, Arata Isozaki, and Daniel Libeskind.

3.2 Turin – The Intersection of Tradition and Innovation

Turin blends its historical architecture with modern designs, showcasing a dynamic and forward-thinking approach to urban development.

- **Key Attractions**:
  - **The Mole Antonelliana**: Originally conceived as a synagogue, this towering structure is a symbol of the city, blending late-19th-century design with modern adaptations, including the **National Cinema Museum** housed inside.
  - **Lingotto Building**: A masterpiece of modernist architecture, this former Fiat factory has been transformed into a center for cultural and commercial activities, complete with a rooftop test track.
  - **The Modern Art Museum (Castello di Rivoli)**: Located in a historic castle, this museum is an important showcase for contemporary art in the region.

4. Artistic Movements in Northern Italy

Northern Italy has long been a center of artistic movements, from the Renaissance to the **Futurism** of the 20th century. Museums and galleries across the region offer insight into the development of Italian art and its global influence.

4.1 Renaissance Art in Northern Italy

- The **Pinacoteca di Brera** in Milan houses one of the most important collections of Italian Renaissance art, with works by **Caravaggio**, **Raphael**, and **Titian**.
- The **Accademia Gallery** in Venice holds an exceptional collection of Venetian Renaissance masterpieces, including works by **Giovanni Bellini** and **Giorgione**.

4.2 Futurism and Modernism in Turin

- **Futurism**, a movement founded in Italy at the beginning of the 20th century, is strongly represented in Turin.

- The **Museo Nazionale del Cinema** and **GAM - Galleria Civica d'Arte Moderna e Contemporanea** showcase the evolution of modern art, from **Futurist paintings** to **contemporary visual arts**.
- **Museo Ettore Fico**: A contemporary art museum in Turin focused on Italian avant-garde and modernist movements, offering a deep dive into the world of **Futurism** and its impact on the visual arts.

5. Preserving Italy's Heritage – Restoration and Conservation

Italy takes immense pride in preserving its cultural heritage, and Northern Italy plays a central role in these efforts. Many landmarks, museums, and historical sites across the region are involved in ongoing conservation and restoration projects to ensure their longevity for future generations.

5.1 The Restoration of Leonardo da Vinci's Works

Milan is home to a number of initiatives aimed at preserving the works of **Leonardo da Vinci**, including the meticulous conservation efforts of **The Last Supper**, which is housed at the **Convent of Santa Maria delle Grazie**. Restoration experts regularly work to maintain the delicate fresco and ensure its brilliance endures.

5.2 Architectural Conservation Projects

Throughout the region, cities like Venice and Milan have undertaken large-scale restoration projects to preserve the architectural integrity of their historic buildings. This includes maintaining the frescoes and sculptures of churches, restoring iconic palaces, and protecting their vibrant urban landscapes from the effects of modernity.

Northern Italy is a living museum of art and architecture, where the past and present coexist harmoniously. From the towering structures of the Renaissance to the bold lines of modern design, the region offers a comprehensive view of Italy's artistic evolution. Whether you are exploring the classical frescoes of Milan, walking through the Venetian palaces, or marveling at contemporary art in Turin, Northern Italy is a destination that will inspire and captivate anyone with an appreciation for fine art and architecture.

4.4 Language and Local Etiquette in Northern Italy

Northern Italy is not just known for its rich history, beautiful landscapes, and remarkable architecture, but also for its distinct cultural identity. Understanding the local language, customs, and etiquette can significantly enhance your experience when traveling through the region. In this section, we explore the languages spoken in

Northern Italy and provide valuable tips on local etiquette that will help you connect with the people and culture during your visit.

1. Languages Spoken in Northern Italy

Northern Italy is a linguistically diverse region, where Italian is the official language but regional languages and dialects add layers of richness to the local identity.

1.1 Standard Italian

- **Location**: Spoken throughout Northern Italy, particularly in urban centers such as Milan, Turin, Venice, and Verona.
- **Key Points**:
    - Italian is the official language of the entire country and is widely spoken and understood in all major cities and tourist areas.
    - Most locals, especially in larger cities, are fluent in Italian, and it's the language used for business, government, and education.
    - While many people working in tourism can understand and speak basic English, speaking a few phrases in Italian can go a long way in creating a positive connection with locals.

1.2 Regional Dialects

- **Lombardy and Milan**: **Milanese** (Milan's dialect), a Lombard variety, is commonly spoken among older generations in local neighborhoods, though Standard Italian is predominant.
- **Veneto and Venice**: **Venetian** is widely spoken in Venice and surrounding areas, though younger people tend to prefer Standard Italian.
- **Piedmont and Turin**: **Piedmontese** is a local dialect spoken by some in Turin, but, again, it's used mainly among older locals.
- **Emilia-Romagna**: **Emilian-Romagnol** dialects are common, especially in smaller towns, though most people are fluent in Italian.
- **Trentino-Alto Adige**: The region has a unique blend of languages, with **German** spoken alongside Italian, especially in towns like Bolzano, where German is an official language.
- **Key Tip**: While regional dialects are an important part of local identity, they are often used in informal settings. In tourist areas and businesses, you'll mostly find that Standard Italian is spoken.

1.3 Understanding Local Expressions

Learning a few basic phrases in Italian can make a big difference, and locals will appreciate your effort to speak their language. Here are some useful phrases:

- **Buongiorno** (Good morning)
- **Ciao** (Hello/Hi)
- **Per favore** (Please)
- **Grazie** (Thank you)
- **Scusi** (Excuse me)
- **Dove si trova...?** (Where is...?)
- **Quanto costa?** (How much does it cost?)

2. Local Etiquette and Customs

Italy is known for its warmth and hospitality, and Northern Italians are generally welcoming and proud of their cultural heritage. To ensure you're respecting local customs, here are some key etiquette tips:

2.1 Greetings and Personal Space

- **Greeting with Formality**: In formal settings (such as when meeting older people or business associates), it's common to greet with a handshake. In informal settings, a kiss on both cheeks is a common greeting among friends and family (starting with the left cheek).
- **Personal Space**: Northern Italians value personal space, and it's important to respect this, especially in public places. While Italians are generally expressive and warm, it's best to avoid being too physically close to strangers.
- **Use of Titles**: Italians are often formal with titles such as **Signore** (Mr.) or **Signora** (Mrs.) when addressing someone for the first time. In more casual settings, first names may be used once rapport is established.

2.2 Dining Etiquette

- **Meal Times**: Italians eat at specific times, and understanding this is important:
  - **Lunch (Pranzo)**: Typically served from 12:30 PM to 2:30 PM.
  - **Dinner (Cena)**: Starts around 7:30 PM to 9:00 PM, though it may be later in larger cities.
  - **Coffee**: In Northern Italy, coffee is typically consumed standing at the bar, especially in Milan and Turin. It's common to order a **caffè** (espresso), and **latte** or **cappuccino** is generally reserved for breakfast.
- **Table Manners**:
  - **Keep your hands on the table** (but not your elbows).
  - **Don't start eating until everyone is served**, and it's polite to wait for the host or the eldest person to begin.
  - **Don't rush**: Meals are often enjoyed at a leisurely pace, with multiple courses. Be sure to take your time.

- **Pasta**: It's typical to twirl pasta with a fork, but avoid using a spoon for assistance.
- **Tipping**: Service charges are often included in the bill (**coperto**), but leaving a tip of around 5–10% for good service is appreciated. In casual settings, tipping is not obligatory.

2.3 Dress Code

- **Fashion-Forward Milan**: Milan, as one of the fashion capitals of the world, sets a high standard for personal style. In Milan, dressing well is a form of respect, and you'll see the locals sporting sleek and sophisticated outfits. While casual dress is fine for sightseeing, avoid wearing overly casual or sloppy clothing when dining in restaurants or entering churches.
- **Church Visits**: When visiting churches or religious sites, it's essential to dress modestly. This typically means covering your shoulders and knees.
- **Seasonal Dressing**: Northern Italy has distinct seasons, and dressing appropriately for the weather is key. Winters can be cold and damp, so packing layers and a warm coat is important. In summer, temperatures can rise, especially in cities like Milan and Verona, so lightweight clothing is essential.

2.4 Punctuality and Business Etiquette

- **Punctuality**: Northern Italians are generally punctual, particularly in business settings. Arriving late to an appointment or meeting is considered disrespectful.
- **Business Meetings**: In professional settings, formal greetings and proper etiquette are highly valued. Addressing individuals by their title and last name (e.g., **Dottore**, **Professore**) shows respect. When conducting business, avoid overly personal topics until you've established rapport.

2.5 Public Behavior

- **Respecting Quiet Spaces**: Northern Italy's public spaces, such as churches, museums, and historical sites, require respectful silence. Talking loudly in such places is considered disrespectful.
- **Queueing**: Italians value order, so always form a line (or **fila**) when waiting for service. Cutting in line is frowned upon, especially in busier cities.

3. Festivals and Traditions

Northern Italy is home to a variety of local festivals and traditions, each with its own cultural significance. Participating in these events gives you a deeper understanding of the region's history and values.

3.1 La Festa della Madonna Bruna (Alessandria)

This traditional festival, celebrated in early July, involves a colorful procession through the streets, marking the city's deep religious roots and sense of community. Locals, dressed in traditional costumes, pay tribute to the **Madonna Bruna**. Visitors can join the festivities, but it's important to be mindful of local religious customs and participate respectfully.

3.2 Carnevale di Venezia (Venice)

One of the most famous festivals in Italy, the **Venice Carnival** (held in February) is marked by elaborate costumes and masks. While participating in this spectacle, it's important to respect local traditions by avoiding behavior that could be seen as disrespectful or disruptive, especially in sacred spaces or during processions.

Understanding and embracing the local language and etiquette when traveling in Northern Italy is key to fostering positive interactions and ensuring a respectful and enjoyable experience. While the region is home to a wide variety of dialects and customs, learning some basic Italian and being mindful of local customs can go a long way in making you feel at home. With its blend of modern and traditional manners, Northern Italy offers an immersive cultural experience for those eager to engage with its people and heritage.

Chapter 5. Outdoor Adventures

5.1 Skiing and Snowboarding in the Dolomites

The **Dolomites**, part of the Southern Alps in Northern Italy, are renowned for their breathtaking beauty and world-class winter sports opportunities. With dramatic mountain peaks, vast ski areas, and picturesque villages, the Dolomites are a must-visit destination for anyone seeking an unforgettable winter adventure. Whether you're an experienced skier or snowboarder, or a beginner looking to explore the slopes, the Dolomites offer an exceptional experience. This section covers the top ski resorts, the range of winter activities, and practical information for an unforgettable trip to this iconic mountain range.

1. Overview of the Dolomites

The Dolomites are a UNESCO World Heritage Site and feature some of the most stunning mountain landscapes in Europe. The region boasts a vast network of ski resorts and trails, making it one of the premier winter destinations in the world. The Dolomites are accessible from several northern Italian cities, with the nearest being **Bolzano**, **Trento**, and **Cortina d'Ampezzo**.

1.1 Ski Resorts in the Dolomites

The Dolomites offer an extensive range of ski resorts, many of which are connected by the **Dolomiti Superski** lift system, one of the largest in the world. Visitors can ski across multiple resorts with a single pass, experiencing diverse landscapes and a variety of slopes. Some of the best resorts include:

- **Cortina d'Ampezzo**: Often considered the most glamorous ski resort in Italy, Cortina is known for its upscale amenities, excellent après-ski scene, and challenging slopes. It has hosted the Winter Olympics and is a top choice for international skiers and snowboarders.
- **Val Gardena**: Famous for its incredible variety of slopes, Val Gardena is part of the **Dolomiti Superski** network. It offers something for everyone—from beginner runs to expert-level black pistes. It also features stunning views of the Sella Ronda circuit, one of the most iconic ski tours in the Dolomites.
- **Alta Badia**: Known for its excellent family-friendly atmosphere, Alta Badia has wide, gentle slopes ideal for beginners and intermediate skiers. The resort also offers a range of gourmet restaurants, making it a unique combination of skiing and fine dining.

- **Madonna di Campiglio**: Located near the **Adamello Brenta Nature Park**, Madonna di Campiglio is a favorite for both skiers and snowboarders. It offers modern facilities, long runs, and off-piste areas for more adventurous riders.
- **Arabba**: Situated in the heart of the Dolomites, Arabba is perfect for advanced skiers who want to challenge themselves with steep, thrilling runs. It is part of the **Sella Ronda**, one of the most famous ski circuits in the world.

1.2 Skiing and Snowboarding Terrain

- **Pistes**: The Dolomites offer more than 1,200 kilometers (750 miles) of ski slopes, catering to skiers and snowboarders of all levels. Whether you're a novice or an expert, there are plenty of options to suit your skill level.
    - **Beginner and Intermediate Slopes**: Resorts like **Alta Badia** and **Val Gardena** offer a range of well-groomed, wide pistes that are perfect for skiers and snowboarders looking to improve their skills.
    - **Advanced and Expert Slopes**: For those seeking a more challenging experience, resorts like **Arabba** and **Cortina d'Ampezzo** feature steep, advanced trails and off-piste terrain.
- **Snowboarding**: The Dolomites also offer excellent facilities for snowboarders, including terrain parks, powder-filled bowls, and challenging off-piste terrain. **Cortina d'Ampezzo** is home to one of Italy's most popular snowboarding parks, while **Val Gardena** and **Arabba** also feature dedicated snowboarding areas.

2. The Sella Ronda – A Legendary Ski Circuit

One of the most famous ski circuits in the world, the **Sella Ronda** is a 26-mile (40 km) loop that connects four major valleys of the Dolomites: **Val Gardena**, **Alta Badia**, **Arabba**, and **Canazei**. The circuit is a must-do for intermediate and advanced skiers, as it allows you to experience the beauty and variety of the Dolomites in a single day. The Sella Ronda is typically done clockwise or counterclockwise, taking you through some of the most stunning mountain passes and offering panoramic views of the surrounding peaks.

- **Key Features**:
    - A wide range of terrain for different skill levels, with both challenging and gentle slopes.
    - Over 25 lifts connecting the four valleys, ensuring minimal wait times.
    - Stunning views of iconic peaks like **Marmolada** (the highest peak in the Dolomites) and the **Sella Group**.

3. Off-Piste and Freeride Skiing

For skiers and snowboarders looking to venture off the beaten path, the Dolomites offer incredible off-piste terrain and freeride opportunities. These areas are best suited for advanced and expert skiers, as they require knowledge of avalanche safety and experience with unmarked slopes.

- **Cortina d'Ampezzo** offers excellent off-piste skiing, including areas around **Tofane** and **Cristallo**.
- **Madonna di Campiglio** is famous for its freeride zones, with terrain that ranges from steep, powder-filled runs to tree-lined descents.
- **Arabba** offers challenging off-piste runs for advanced skiers, including steep couloirs and glacial terrain.

Guided tours are recommended for those who want to explore off-piste areas safely.

4. Skiing for All Ages – Family-Friendly Resorts

The Dolomites are not just for expert skiers—they also offer excellent options for families and children. Resorts like **Alta Badia** and **Val Gardena** are known for their family-friendly atmosphere, with ski schools, kid-friendly slopes, and child-friendly accommodations. In addition to skiing, many resorts offer activities like snowshoeing, tobogganing, and ice skating, making it an ideal destination for families with children of all ages.

- **Kids' Ski Schools**: The Dolomites are home to several ski schools with programs for children, ranging from beginner to advanced levels.
- **Snow Parks**: Many resorts feature snow parks specifically designed for younger skiers and snowboarders, with gentle slopes and fun obstacles to help them improve their skills.

5. Après-Ski in the Dolomites

After a day on the slopes, the Dolomites offer plenty of opportunities to unwind and enjoy the après-ski scene. From cozy mountain huts to lively town centers, you can enjoy the region's famous hospitality, delicious food, and local .

- **Cortina d'Ampezzo** is the place to be for an upscale après-ski experience, with chic bars, stylish lounges, and gourmet dining options.
- **Val Gardena** offers a more relaxed après-ski atmosphere, with plenty of traditional taverns and live music.

- **Alta Badia** has a renowned après-ski scene, where visitors can enjoy a warm drink or aperitif after a day on the slopes while soaking in the breathtaking mountain views.

6. Best Time to Visit for Skiing and Snowboarding

The best time for skiing and snowboarding in the Dolomites is typically from **December to April**, with **January and February** offering the most reliable snow conditions. However, the region can also offer skiing later in the season, especially at higher altitudes.

- **December to February**: The peak ski season, with the best snow conditions and the busiest crowds.
- **March to April**: A great time for skiing, especially for those who enjoy spring skiing with milder temperatures. The slopes are less crowded, and resorts still offer good snow coverage at higher elevations.

7. Practical Tips for Skiing and Snowboarding in the Dolomites

- **Lift Passes**: The **Dolomiti Superski Pass** allows access to all the major resorts in the region, including Cortina, Val Gardena, and Alta Badia. It's the best way to explore the vast ski areas.
- **Renting Equipment**: Equipment rentals are available at most resorts, and you can easily rent skis, snowboards, helmets, and even clothing.
- **Lessons**: Ski schools are available at every major resort, offering group and private lessons for all levels.
- **Safety**: Always check avalanche forecasts and follow local guidelines when skiing off-piste. It's recommended to take a **Guided Freeride Tour** for those exploring unmarked areas.

Skiing and snowboarding in the Dolomites offer an unparalleled experience, combining world-class facilities, stunning natural beauty, and a wide range of terrain suited to all levels of expertise. Whether you're a seasoned skier looking for challenging runs, a beginner ready to learn, or a family seeking a winter holiday, the Dolomites provide an extraordinary destination for outdoor adventure in Northern Italy.

5.2 Hiking and Mountain Climbing in the Dolomites

The **Dolomites**, renowned for their striking peaks, valleys, and alpine meadows, offer some of the most spectacular hiking and mountain climbing experiences in the world. With trails ranging from easy walks to challenging summit ascents, this region attracts outdoor enthusiasts of all levels. Whether you're seeking a leisurely hike or an ambitious climb, the Dolomites provide an unforgettable experience, with awe-inspiring landscapes and an opportunity to immerse yourself in nature. This section covers the best hiking trails, mountain climbing routes, and practical advice for those venturing into the heart of the Dolomites.

1. Overview of Hiking and Mountain Climbing in the Dolomites

The Dolomites are a UNESCO World Heritage Site, and with good reason. The rugged, jagged peaks, expansive valleys, and alpine lakes create a paradise for outdoor enthusiasts. The region offers more than **1,000 kilometers** of hiking trails, ranging from easy strolls to some of the most demanding climbs in Europe.

- **Terrain Variety**: From lush meadows and peaceful lakes to high-altitude alpine landscapes and rocky ridgelines, the Dolomites offer a wide variety of terrains that make for diverse and stunning hiking experiences.
- **Access Points**: The Dolomites are easily accessible from several towns in Northern Italy, including **Bolzano**, **Cortina d'Ampezzo**, **Canazei**, **Ortisei**, and **Selva di Val Gardena**. Many of these towns offer gondolas and cable cars to help you access higher altitudes quickly, enabling you to explore further without long ascents.

2. Best Hiking Trails in the Dolomites

2.1 Tre Cime di Lavaredo (Three Peaks of Lavaredo)

- **Location**: Near **Dobbiaco** in the eastern Dolomites.
- **Distance**: 10 kilometers (6.2 miles).
- **Duration**: 4–5 hours.
- **Difficulty**: Moderate.

The Tre Cime di Lavaredo are perhaps the most iconic peaks in the Dolomites, and the hike around them is equally spectacular. The circular route takes you past the three towering peaks, offering breathtaking views of the surrounding valleys. The trail is well-marked and accessible for most hikers, with the option to shorten the hike by taking the shuttle bus to the Rifugio Auronzo (a mountain hut located close to the starting point). Along the way, hikers can marvel at the dramatic landscape, with rugged cliffs, alpine meadows, and crystal-clear lakes.

- **Key Features**:
  - Stunning views of the **Tre Cime** (Three Peaks).
  - The opportunity to visit mountain huts (rifugi) for a rest and a meal.
  - Rich wildlife, including marmots, ibex, and eagles.

2.2 Alta Via 1 (The Dolomites High Route 1)

- **Location**: Runs from **Lake Braies** in the north to **Belluno** in the south.
- **Distance**: 150 kilometers (93 miles).
- **Duration**: 10–12 days.
- **Difficulty**: Moderate to challenging.

For serious hikers, the **Alta Via 1** is one of the most popular long-distance routes in the Dolomites. It traverses the region from north to south, passing through high-altitude ridgelines, alpine meadows, and rocky valleys. Hikers can stay in mountain huts along the way, making it possible to complete the entire route over several days. The trail offers panoramic views of some of the Dolomites' most famous peaks, such as **Tofane**, **Marmolada**, and **Civetta**.

- **Key Features**:
    - High-altitude hiking with varied terrain.
    - The opportunity to explore remote corners of the Dolomites.
    - Access to refuges and guesthouses where hikers can rest.

2.3 Seceda and the Alpe di Siusi

- **Location**: Near **Ortisei** in the Val Gardena valley.
- **Distance**: 5 kilometers (3.1 miles) to 20 kilometers (12.4 miles), depending on the route.
- **Duration**: 2–6 hours.
- **Difficulty**: Easy to moderate.

This area offers some of the most beautiful hikes in the Dolomites, with lush meadows, rolling hills, and impressive mountain views. The **Seceda** area is famous for its views of the **Sella Group** and **Langkofel**, while the **Alpe di Siusi** is the largest high-altitude alpine plateau in Europe, ideal for gentle hikes. The gentle slopes and serene atmosphere make it a great spot for families and beginners, as well as for experienced hikers looking for a relaxed day on the trails.

- **Key Features**:
    - Breathtaking views of the **Sella** and **Langkofel** mountain ranges.
    - Excellent conditions for hiking and photography.
    - A variety of short and long routes, making it suitable for all levels.

2.4 Lago di Sorapis

- **Location**: Near **Cortina d'Ampezzo** in the Dolomites.
- **Distance**: 12 kilometers (7.5 miles).

- **Duration**: 5–6 hours.
- **Difficulty**: Moderate.

The hike to **Lago di Sorapis** offers a tranquil and scenic experience. The trail takes you through forests, alpine meadows, and rocky outcrops to reach the turquoise-blue lake. The color of the water is especially striking, set against the backdrop of towering cliffs. The hike is challenging due to the rugged terrain and some steep sections, but the stunning lake at the end makes the effort worthwhile.

- **Key Features**:
    - The remarkable turquoise color of **Lago di Sorapis**.
    - Solitude and serenity, as the trail is less crowded than others.
    - Breathtaking views of surrounding peaks like **Sorapis** and **Tofane**.

3. Mountain Climbing in the Dolomites

The Dolomites are also a top destination for experienced mountain climbers. With their rugged, jagged peaks, the Dolomites offer some of the most famous and challenging climbing routes in Europe. Many of the climbing routes have historical significance, with early 20th-century climbers leaving their mark on the region.

3.1 The Via Ferrata

- **Description**: Via Ferrata is a type of protected climbing route that combines hiking with rock climbing. These routes are equipped with cables, ladders, and bridges, making them accessible to climbers without specialized rock-climbing skills.

Some of the most famous via ferrata routes in the Dolomites include:

- **Via Ferrata degli Alpini** (Cortina d'Ampezzo): A relatively easy route that offers stunning views of the surrounding mountains.
- **Via Ferrata di Punta Fiames** (near Cortina d'Ampezzo): A more challenging route that includes steep sections and exposed ridgelines.
- **Via Ferrata Lipella** (Cinque Torri): This is one of the more famous via ferrata routes in the Dolomites, taking climbers up the iconic **Cinque Torri** towers.

3.2 The Marmolada Summit

- **Location**: **Marmolada**, the highest peak in the Dolomites (3,342 meters or 10,965 feet).
- **Route Difficulty**: High, requires mountaineering experience.

The **Marmolada** is known as the "Queen of the Dolomites" and offers some of the most rewarding and demanding climbs in the region. Reaching the summit requires a glacier ascent, which should only be attempted by experienced climbers with proper equipment. The panoramic views from the top are incredible, stretching across the entire Dolomite mountain range.

4. Practical Information for Hiking and Mountain Climbing

- **Best Time to Visit**: Hiking and climbing are best done from **June to September**, with the summer months offering the most favorable weather conditions. In winter, the trails may be covered in snow and ice, making them dangerous without specialized equipment.
- **Weather**: The weather in the Dolomites can change rapidly, so hikers and climbers should be prepared for all conditions. Always check the forecast before heading out.
- **Equipment**: For hiking, sturdy boots, weather-appropriate clothing, and a map are essential. For via ferrata or climbing, a helmet, harness, and carabiners are necessary. Many mountain huts rent equipment for those new to climbing.
- **Guides and Refuges**: Experienced mountain guides are recommended for challenging routes, and refuges (mountain huts) are scattered throughout the region, offering food, drink, and accommodation.

Whether you're a novice hiker looking for a scenic walk or an experienced mountaineer eager to conquer challenging peaks, the Dolomites provide a vast array of options for outdoor adventure. The combination of stunning landscapes, well-marked trails, and world-class climbing routes makes the Dolomites one of the best destinations for hiking and mountain climbing in Europe. With proper preparation, respect for the terrain, and a spirit of adventure, the Dolomites are sure to provide an unforgettable experience.

5.3 Cycling Trails in Northern Italy

Northern Italy is an exceptional destination for cycling enthusiasts, offering a diverse range of landscapes, from rolling vineyards and lakeside paths to rugged mountains and historic cities. With its extensive network of cycling routes, ranging from leisurely bike paths to challenging mountain climbs, the region is a paradise for both casual cyclists and competitive riders. Whether you're looking to explore the beauty of the Italian countryside or tackle some of the most famous climbs in the cycling world, Northern Italy has something to offer.

1. Overview of Cycling in Northern Italy

Cycling in Northern Italy is well-established, with dedicated bike paths, mountain trails, and famous routes that attract cyclists from around the world. The region benefits from a mild climate, particularly in spring and autumn, making it an ideal destination for cycling. Major cycling events, like the **Giro d'Italia** (Italy's premier cycling race), further highlight the importance of cycling in the country's culture. Many of the routes here pass through UNESCO World Heritage sites, picturesque villages, and world-famous landmarks, providing an unforgettable cycling experience.

- **Cycling Seasons**: The best time to cycle in Northern Italy is from **April to October**, when temperatures are mild and precipitation is minimal. Summer months (June–August) can be hot, especially in lowland areas, while spring and autumn offer cooler conditions and fewer crowds.

- **Cycling Routes and Terrain**: Northern Italy offers a variety of terrain for all levels of cyclists, including flat routes for leisurely rides, rolling hills for intermediate cyclists, and challenging mountain routes for experienced riders.

2. Popular Cycling Trails in Northern Italy

2.1 The Veneto Cycle Route (Veneto Region)

- **Location**: From **Padua** to **Venice**, passing through **Treviso** and the **Prosecco Hills**.
- **Distance**: 135 kilometers (84 miles).
- **Duration**: 2–3 days.
- **Difficulty**: Easy to moderate.

The **Veneto Cycle Route** is a beautiful ride through some of Northern Italy's most picturesque landscapes, passing through charming towns, vineyards, and historical landmarks. Starting in **Padua**, the route leads cyclists toward the historic city of **Venice**, offering plenty of opportunities for sightseeing along the way.

- **Key Features**:
    - Scenic views of the **Prosecco Hills**, where the famous sparkling is produced.
    - Quiet, well-maintained bike paths that are suitable for all levels of cyclists.
    - Opportunities to stop in quaint villages for food, , and historical exploration.

2.2 The Lake Garda Cycle Path (Lago di Garda)

- **Location**: Around **Lake Garda**, including towns like **Riva del Garda**, **Malcesine**, and **Sirmione**.
- **Distance**: 140 kilometers (87 miles).
- **Duration**: 1–3 days, depending on the route chosen.
- **Difficulty**: Easy to moderate.

Lake Garda, the largest lake in Italy, offers one of the most scenic cycling routes in the country. The **Lake Garda Cycle Path** follows the shoreline, passing through charming lakeside towns and offering stunning views of the surrounding mountains. Cyclists can enjoy leisurely rides along the flat sections, while more adventurous routes offer some climbing, especially near the northern part of the lake.

- **Key Features**:
    - Panoramic views of **Lake Garda** and surrounding mountains.
    - Quaint towns with historical landmarks, such as **Sirmione** and **Malcesine**.
    - A mix of easy lakeside routes and more challenging climbs, especially near the northern end.

2.3 The Dolomites Cycling Routes (Dolomiti Region)

- **Location**: The Dolomites, including towns like **Cortina d'Ampezzo, Canazei**, and **Selva di Val Gardena**.
- **Distance**: Varies, with several famous routes such as the **Sella Ronda** loop (55 kilometers) and the **Maratona dles Dolomites** race route (138 kilometers).
- **Duration**: 1–3 days.
- **Difficulty**: Moderate to difficult.

The **Dolomites** are a haven for cycling enthusiasts, offering both stunning scenery and challenging climbs. Famous routes like the **Sella Ronda**, part of the annual **Maratona dles Dolomites** race, attract cyclists from all over the world. With mountain passes like **Passo Pordoi, Passo Sella**, and **Passo Gardena**, riders can enjoy breathtaking views while tackling some of the most famous climbs in cycling.

- **Key Features**:
    - Legendary mountain passes known for their appearance in the **Giro d'Italia**.
    - Spectacular alpine scenery, including rocky peaks, meadows, and mountain lakes.
    - A variety of routes suitable for both amateur and professional cyclists.

2.4 The Francigena Via (Tuscany to Piedmont)

- **Location**: From **Pavia** to **Aosta**, through the **Langhe Hills** and **Tuscany**.
- **Distance**: 300 kilometers (186 miles).
- **Duration**: 4–5 days.
- **Difficulty**: Moderate.

The **Via Francigena** is an ancient pilgrimage route that stretches from **Canterbury**, England, to **Rome**. This modern-day cycling path takes riders through Northern Italy's rolling hills and historic villages. The route traverses the **Langhe** -producing region and the scenic **Tuscany** landscape, providing an immersive cultural and cycling experience.

- **Key Features**:
    - Rich history, as the route is part of the historic **Via Francigena** pilgrimage.
    - Cycling through vineyards, medieval villages, and UNESCO-protected landscapes.
    - The possibility to explore the famous regions of **Langhe** and **Monferrato**.

2.5 The Valtellina Cycle Path (Lombardy Region)

- **Location**: Along the **Adda River** from **Tirano** to **Lecco**.
- **Distance**: 120 kilometers (74 miles).
- **Duration**: 2–3 days.
- **Difficulty**: Easy to moderate.

The **Valtellina Cycle Path** is a popular route that follows the **Adda River**, offering scenic views of the Alps and valleys. The path is relatively flat, making it ideal for cyclists looking for an easy, relaxing ride through stunning landscapes. The route passes through charming villages, vineyards, and nature reserves, providing plenty of opportunities for rest and exploration.

- **Key Features**:
    - Flat terrain, making it suitable for cyclists of all levels.
    - Views of the **Orobie Alps** and the **Adda River**.
    - Stops at charming towns like **Tirano**, **Sondrio**, and **Lecco**, with plenty of opportunities to sample local food and .

3. Cycling Events in Northern Italy

Northern Italy also plays host to several prestigious cycling events, attracting cyclists from around the world. Some of the most famous events include:

- **Giro d'Italia**: One of the most important cycling races in the world, held annually. The Dolomites and the Alps feature prominently in the race's route, offering spectacular views and challenging climbs.
- **Maratona dles Dolomites**: A challenging road race through the Dolomites, attracting amateur and professional cyclists alike.
- **Gran Fondo Stelvio Santini**: A mass-participation cycling event that takes riders on a challenging route through the **Stelvio Pass**, one of the highest and most famous passes in Italy.

4. Practical Tips for Cycling in Northern Italy

- **Equipment**: Be sure to bring a good-quality bike, especially if you plan to tackle the more challenging mountain routes. Many towns and cities offer bike rental services, and some specialized shops also rent out electric bikes, which are particularly useful on steep climbs.
- **Bike Paths and Roads**: Northern Italy is well-equipped with dedicated bike paths, especially in urban areas and along lakesides. When cycling on roads, be cautious and follow local traffic regulations.
- **Weather**: Check the weather forecast before setting out. In the mountains, weather conditions can change rapidly, so be prepared for both warm and cold temperatures, even in summer.
- **Safety**: Always wear a helmet and be aware of your surroundings. Many of the mountain roads can be narrow and winding, so extra caution is required.

Cycling in Northern Italy offers an incredible combination of adventure, natural beauty, and cultural exploration. Whether you're cycling around **Lake Garda**, tackling the iconic climbs of the **Dolomites**, or enjoying a more leisurely route through **Tuscany**, there is no shortage of stunning routes for cyclists of all abilities. With well-maintained paths, a rich cycling culture, and unforgettable landscapes, Northern Italy is a top destination for cycling enthusiasts from around the world.

5.4 Exploring the Lakes Region

The **Lakes Region** of Northern Italy is one of the most captivating and scenic areas in the country. With its pristine waters, charming lakeside towns, and dramatic mountain backdrops, this region offers a perfect combination of outdoor activities and natural beauty. From the glimmering shores of **Lake Como** to the serene landscapes of **Lake**

Maggiore, each lake presents unique opportunities for adventure, relaxation, and exploration. Whether you're seeking water-based activities, hiking trails, or simply want to enjoy the lakeside ambiance, the Lakes Region has something for everyone.

1. Overview of the Lakes Region

Northern Italy is home to several stunning lakes, each with its own character and attractions. The region is characterized by a mix of mountainous terrain, lush forests, and picturesque villages that dot the lake shores. The lakes are easily accessible from major cities like Milan, Verona, and Turin, making it a convenient destination for both day trips and longer stays.

- **Famous Lakes in the Region**:
    - **Lake Como**
    - **Lake Garda**
    - **Lake Maggiore**
    - **Lake Iseo**
    - **Lake Orta**

The Lakes Region has long been a favorite destination for royalty, artists, and celebrities, with luxurious villas and historic towns offering a glimpse into the region's rich cultural heritage.

2. Key Lakes to Explore

2.1 Lake Como

- **Location**: Lombardy region, near the Swiss border.
- **Size**: 146 square kilometers (57 square miles).
- **Main Towns**: Como, Bellagio, Varenna, Menaggio.
- **Highlights**:
    - **Villa del Balbianello**: A historic villa with beautiful gardens, famous for being featured in James Bond movies.
    - **Boat tours**: A great way to explore the lakeside towns and villas.
    - **Walking and cycling paths**: Scenic routes around the lake and up into the mountains.

Lake Como is arguably the most famous of Northern Italy's lakes, known for its stunning natural beauty and glamorous reputation. Surrounded by mountains and dotted with picturesque villages, Lake Como offers numerous opportunities for water sports, boat tours, and hiking. The charming towns around the lake, like **Bellagio** and **Varenna**, are perfect for leisurely strolls, with cobblestone streets, lovely cafes, and beautiful gardens.

2.2 Lake Garda

- **Location**: Between the regions of **Lombardy**, **Veneto**, and **Trentino-Alto Adige/Südtirol**.
- **Size**: 370 square kilometers (143 square miles).
- **Main Towns**: Sirmione, Riva del Garda, Malcesine, Desenzano del Garda.
- **Highlights**:
  - **Grotte di Catullo**: Ancient Roman ruins located in **Sirmione**.
  - **Riva del Garda**: A hub for windsurfing and sailing enthusiasts.
  - **Monte Baldo**: A mountain with panoramic views, accessible by cable car.

Lake Garda is Italy's largest lake and offers diverse activities ranging from sailing and windsurfing to hiking and cycling. The surrounding landscape includes vineyards, olive groves, and steep cliffs that create dramatic views. The town of **Sirmione**, with its medieval castle and Roman ruins, is one of the most popular destinations on the lake, while the northern part of the lake is known for its adventure sports.

2.3 Lake Maggiore

- **Location**: Shared by the regions of **Piedmont** and **Lombardy**, as well as Switzerland.
- **Size**: 212 square kilometers (82 square miles).
- **Main Towns**: Stresa, Verbania, Arona, Cannobio.
- **Highlights**:
  - **Borromean Islands**: A group of islands with historic villas and lush gardens, accessible by boat from **Stresa**.
  - **Mottarone**: A mountain offering hiking trails and panoramic views of the lake.
  - **Villa Taranto**: A botanical garden located in **Verbania**.

Lake Maggiore is known for its calm, blue waters and the stunning **Borromean Islands**. The lake is also home to several historic villas, charming lakeside towns, and hiking opportunities. It is less touristy than Lake Como, providing a more relaxed experience for visitors. The mountain of **Mottarone** offers spectacular views of the surrounding area, while **Villa Taranto** is a must-visit for garden lovers.

2.4 Lake Iseo

- **Location**: Lombardy region, between **Bergamo** and **Brescia**.
- **Size**: 65.3 square kilometers (25.2 square miles).
- **Main Towns**: Iseo, Sarnico, Pisogne.
- **Highlights**:

- **Monte Isola**: The largest lake island in Italy, known for its quaint villages and walking trails.
- **Lovere**: A beautiful lakeside town with medieval architecture.
- **Franciacorta Vineyards**: A -producing region near the lake.

Lake Iseo is one of the lesser-known lakes in Northern Italy, but it is a hidden gem. It is famous for **Monte Isola**, an island in the middle of the lake that can be reached by boat. The lake offers a peaceful atmosphere and a chance to explore charming villages, vineyards, and natural beauty. It is an excellent destination for hiking, cycling, and boat tours.

2.5 Lake Orta

- **Location**: Piedmont region, near Lake Maggiore.
- **Size**: 18.2 square kilometers (7.0 square miles).
- **Main Towns**: Orta San Giulio, Pella, Omegna.
- **Highlights**:
    - **Isola San Giulio**: A small, tranquil island with a monastery.
    - **Orta San Giulio**: A picturesque lakeside town with medieval buildings and cobblestone streets.
    - **Mottarone**: Offering views of both Lake Orta and Lake Maggiore.

Lake Orta is a small, serene lake that is perfect for visitors looking for a more tranquil and intimate experience. The town of **Orta San Giulio** is charming, with narrow alleys and lovely cafés, while **Isola San Giulio** offers a peaceful retreat for visitors. The lake is less crowded than other lakes in the region, making it ideal for relaxation and reflection.

3. Outdoor Activities in the Lakes Region

The Lakes Region offers numerous outdoor activities, particularly for nature lovers and adventure seekers.

- **Water Sports**: All of the lakes are perfect for water-based activities such as boating, sailing, windsurfing, kayaking, and swimming. Lake Garda, in particular, is famous for its excellent windsurfing conditions.

- **Hiking and Trekking**: The lakes are surrounded by mountains, offering a range of hiking opportunities. Trails around **Lake Como** and **Lake Garda** take you through lush forests, steep hills, and along cliffs with incredible views of the water.

- **Cycling**: Many of the lakes, particularly **Lake Garda** and **Lake Como**, have well-maintained cycling paths that follow the shoreline. For more experienced cyclists, the mountains around the lakes offer challenging climbs and scenic routes.

4. Practical Tips for Exploring the Lakes Region

- **Transportation**: While the Lakes Region is well-connected by train and bus, renting a car can provide more flexibility, especially for reaching more remote areas or enjoying scenic drives around the lakes. Boats are an excellent way to travel between towns on the lakes.

- **Best Time to Visit**: The peak tourist season is during the summer months (June–August), but visiting in the **spring** or **autumn** offers a quieter experience, with pleasant weather and fewer crowds.

- **Accommodations**: The region offers a wide range of accommodations, from luxurious lakeside resorts to charming B&Bs and historic hotels. Many of the towns have hotels with stunning views of the lakes.

Exploring the Lakes Region of Northern Italy is an unforgettable experience, offering a perfect blend of natural beauty, outdoor activities, and cultural exploration. Whether you're looking to enjoy the serenity of **Lake Orta**, indulge in water sports on **Lake Garda**, or wander through the picturesque towns of **Lake Como**, there's something for every type of traveler. With its stunning landscapes, charming towns, and wealth of activities, the Lakes Region is a must-visit destination for anyone traveling to Northern Italy.

Chapter 6. Regional Highlights

6.1 Lombardy

Lombardy is one of Italy's most dynamic and culturally rich regions, located in the heart of Northern Italy. It is not only home to **Milan**, Italy's economic and fashion capital, but also boasts a wealth of natural beauty, historical landmarks, and charming towns. From the world-renowned **Lake Como** to the majestic **Alps**, Lombardy offers a diverse mix of attractions, making it a top destination for travelers. The region's blend of modernity and tradition, combined with its rich cultural heritage, ensures there's something for everyone.

1. Overview of Lombardy

- **Capital**: Milan
- **Location**: Northern Italy, bordering Switzerland to the north and several other Italian regions, including Piedmont, Emilia-Romagna, and Veneto.
- **Area**: 23,861 square kilometers (9,207 square miles)
- **Population**: Approximately 10 million (making it one of the most populous regions in Italy)
- **Famous for**: Fashion, design, art, lakes, Alps, and culinary excellence.

Lombardy is an economic powerhouse, accounting for a significant portion of Italy's GDP due to its industrial output, finance, and trade. While Milan is known worldwide for its business and fashion industries, Lombardy also offers tranquil countryside landscapes, picturesque lakes, and charming medieval towns. Its geography is diverse, featuring lush plains, rolling hills, alpine peaks, and pristine lakes.

2. Major Attractions in Lombardy

2.1 Milan – The Fashion and Design Capital

- **Location**: Central Lombardy
- **Highlights**:
    - **Duomo di Milano**: One of the most iconic cathedrals in the world. Visitors can climb to the rooftop for panoramic views of the city.
    - **Galleria Vittorio Emanuele II**: A historic shopping gallery home to luxury brands.
    - **Sforza Castle**: A Renaissance fortress with museums and beautiful courtyards.
    - **The Last Supper by Leonardo da Vinci**: A world-renowned fresco housed in the **Santa Maria delle Grazie** church.
    - **Fashion District**: Famous for high-end shopping, featuring designers such as **Versace**, **Gucci**, and **Prada**.

Milan is a global city known for its fashion, design, and finance sectors. In addition to being Italy's economic hub, it boasts impressive architectural landmarks, including the Gothic-style **Duomo** and **Galleria Vittorio Emanuele II**, a shopping mall housed in an ornate 19th-century building. The city also has a thriving arts scene, with iconic museums like **Pinacoteca di Brera** and **Teatro alla Scala**.

2.2 Lake Como

- **Location**: Northern Lombardy, near the Swiss border
- **Highlights**:
    - **Bellagio**: A picturesque town often called the "Pearl of Lake Como."
    - **Villa del Balbianello**: A beautiful villa with stunning gardens, famous for being featured in James Bond films.
    - **Varenna**: A charming lakeside village with cobblestone streets and a scenic waterfront.
    - **Boat Tours**: Explore the lake's crystal-clear waters and visit the many villas and towns that line the shoreline.
    - **Hiking Trails**: Explore the mountains surrounding the lake for breathtaking views.

Lake Como is one of Italy's most famous and picturesque lakes, renowned for its crystal-clear waters and the surrounding mountains. The town of **Bellagio** is particularly well-known for its charm, while **Villa del Balbianello** attracts visitors from around the world for its beauty and cinematic fame. The region offers an array of activities such as hiking, boating, and visiting historic villas.

2.3 Bergamo

- **Location**: Eastern Lombardy, near the foothills of the Alps
- **Highlights**:
  - **Città Alta (Upper Town)**: A medieval town with cobblestone streets, ancient walls, and panoramic views.
  - **Piazza Vecchia**: The heart of the historic center, featuring the **Palazzo della Ragione** and **Torre Civica**.
  - **Basilica di Santa Maria Maggiore**: A stunning church with beautiful frescoes.
  - **Accademia Carrara**: An art museum featuring works by Italian masters like **Caravaggio** and **Raffaello**.

Bergamo is a charming town divided into two parts: the lower town, which is modern and bustling, and the **Città Alta**, the upper medieval town that offers visitors a journey back in time. The cobbled streets, ancient gates, and picturesque squares are just a few of the town's many attractions.

2.4 Franciacorta Region

- **Location**: Central Lombardy, between **Brescia** and **Lake Iseo**
- **Highlights**:
  - **Franciacorta Vineyards**: Famous for producing high-quality sparkling s, similar to Champagne.
  - **ries and Tours**: Visit local ries to taste the region's renowned **Franciacorta DOCG s**.
  - **Brescia**: The nearby city known for its historical sites, including the **Roman Forum** and the **Santa Giulia Museum**.

The **Franciacorta** region is known for its beautiful vineyards that produce world-class sparkling s. This area, situated between **Lake Iseo** and **Brescia**, offers visitors an opportunity to explore picturesque ries and taste locally produced s.

2.5 The Alps – Skiing and Mountaineering

- **Location**: Northern Lombardy, bordering Switzerland
- **Highlights**:
  - **Madesimo**: A popular ski resort offering excellent slopes for all skill levels.

- **Livigno**: Known for its duty-free shopping and vibrant après-ski culture.
- **Bormio**: Famous for its thermal baths and ski slopes.
- **Stelvio Pass**: One of the highest mountain passes in Europe, known for its challenging roads and spectacular views.

Lombardy's northern borders are dominated by the **Alps**, offering world-class skiing, mountaineering, and hiking. Resorts like **Madesimo**, **Livigno**, and **Bormio** provide visitors with opportunities to enjoy snow sports during the winter months, while the summer months offer incredible hiking routes and mountain biking trails.

3. Cultural Highlights of Lombardy

Lombardy is rich in cultural heritage, from historical monuments and art galleries to the vibrant traditions of local towns.

- **Opera and Ballet**: Milan's **Teatro alla Scala** is one of the most famous opera houses in the world, regularly hosting international performances.
- **Art and Architecture**: Lombardy boasts several UNESCO World Heritage Sites, including **Crespi d'Adda**, a model village from the industrial era, and the **Sacri Monti of Piedmont and Lombardy**, a series of sacred mountains with chapels and sanctuaries.
- **Cuisine**: Lombardy is known for hearty dishes such as **risotto alla Milanese** (saffron-infused rice) and **ossobuco** (braised veal shanks), as well as rich cheeses like **Gorgonzola** and **Grana Padano**.

4. Practical Information for Visiting Lombardy

- **Best Time to Visit**:

  - **Spring (April–June)**: Pleasant temperatures and fewer tourists.
  - **Autumn (September–October)**: Mild weather, ideal for outdoor activities and harvest season.
  - **Winter (December–February)**: Perfect for skiing and snow activities in the Alps.
- **Getting Around**: Lombardy has an excellent transportation network, including high-speed trains, buses, and ferries for lake transport. **Milan** is well-connected to other Italian cities and European destinations via its airports (Malpensa, Linate) and central train stations.

Lombardy is a region of contrasts, where cutting-edge modernity meets centuries-old traditions. Whether you're exploring the cultural treasures of **Milan**, relaxing by the shimmering waters of **Lake Como**, skiing in the **Alps**, or savoring local s in **Franciacorta**, Lombardy offers an unforgettable experience. Its combination of history, natural beauty, and modern attractions makes it a must-visit destination in Northern Italy.

6.2 Veneto

Veneto is one of the most captivating regions of Northern Italy, known for its rich history, scenic landscapes, and cultural landmarks. From the iconic city of **Venice** to the rolling hills of **Valpolicella** and the majestic **Dolomites**, Veneto offers a diverse array of attractions for every type of traveler. The region is steeped in centuries of art, architecture, and tradition, making it a perfect blend of history and natural beauty.

1. Overview of Veneto

- **Capital**: Venice
- **Location**: Northeastern Italy, bordered by **Friuli Venezia Giulia** to the east, **Trentino-Alto Adige** to the north, **Lombardy** to the west, and the **Adriatic Sea** to the south.
- **Area**: 18,399 square kilometers (7,107 square miles)
- **Population**: Approximately 5 million

- **Famous for**: Venice, art and architecture, Prosecco, medieval towns, and the **Dolomites**.

Veneto's geographic variety spans from the picturesque **Venetian Lagoon** and historical cities to the breathtaking mountain peaks of the **Dolomites**. Its cities, particularly **Venice**, are renowned worldwide for their beauty and cultural significance. Veneto is also famous for its s, including the sparkling **Prosecco** and rich **Valpolicella** reds.

2. Major Attractions in Veneto

2.1 Venice – The City of Canals

- **Location**: Southern Veneto, on the Adriatic Sea
- **Highlights**:
    - **St. Mark's Basilica**: A masterpiece of Byzantine architecture, known for its opulent mosaics and golden altarpiece.
    - **Rialto Bridge**: One of Venice's most famous landmarks, offering stunning views of the Grand Canal.
    - **Doge's Palace**: A symbol of Venice's political power during the Republic of Venice.
    - **Gondola Rides**: An iconic Venetian experience that offers a unique view of the city from its canals.
    - **Murano and Burano Islands**: Famous for glass-making (Murano) and colorful fishing villages (Burano).

Venice, with its labyrinth of canals, cobblestone streets, and grand palaces, is one of the most unique cities in the world. Whether you're admiring the mosaics in **St. Mark's Basilica**, cruising along the Grand Canal on a gondola, or exploring the islands of **Murano** and **Burano**, Venice offers endless cultural and historical treasures. The city is a UNESCO World Heritage Site and a must-see destination for any traveler to Veneto.

2.2 Verona – Shakespeare's City of Love

- **Location**: Eastern Veneto, along the Adige River
- **Highlights**:
    - **Arena di Verona**: A Roman amphitheater still used for concerts and opera performances.
    - **Juliet's House**: The famed balcony from Shakespeare's **Romeo and Juliet**.
    - **Piazza delle Erbe**: A lively square surrounded by historic buildings and markets.

- **Castelvecchio**: A medieval fortress housing an art museum.
- **Piazza Bra**: A grand square near the Arena, often filled with cafes and restaurants.

Verona, often associated with **Romeo and Juliet**, is a romantic and historically rich city. Its **Arena** is one of the best-preserved Roman amphitheaters in Italy and still hosts world-class performances. Verona's picturesque streets, beautiful medieval buildings, and vibrant piazzas make it a charming destination, particularly for lovers of art, history, and literature.

2.3 Padua – The City of Saints

- **Location**: Western Veneto, near the **Brenta River**
- **Highlights**:
    - **Basilica di Sant'Antonio**: One of Italy's most important pilgrimage sites, dedicated to St. Anthony of Padua.
    - **Scrovegni Chapel**: A small chapel known for its stunning frescoes by **Giotto**.
    - **Prato della Valle**: One of the largest squares in Europe, surrounded by statues and gardens.
    - **Palazzo della Ragione**: A medieval palace with a large frescoed hall and panoramic views of the city.

Padua is an ancient city with a vibrant history. Its most famous landmark, the **Basilica di Sant'Antonio**, attracts pilgrims from all over the world. The **Scrovegni Chapel**, with its stunning frescoes by **Giotto**, is a must-see for art lovers. The city is also home to **Padua University**, one of the oldest universities in the world, adding to the city's cultural and intellectual importance.

2.4 Lake Garda – Veneto's Beautiful Lakeside Escape

- **Location**: Bordering **Lombardy**, **Veneto**, and **Trentino-Alto Adige**
- **Highlights**:
    - **Sirmione**: A charming lakeside town with a medieval castle and Roman ruins.
    - **Riva del Garda**: A hub for water sports and outdoor activities.
    - **Malcesine**: A picturesque town with a medieval castle and cable car access to **Monte Baldo**.
    - **Gardone Riviera**: Known for its botanical gardens and the **Vittoriale degli Italiani**, the former home of poet **Gabriele D'Annunzio**.

Lake Garda, the largest lake in Italy, straddles Veneto, Lombardy, and Trentino-Alto Adige. It offers a blend of outdoor adventure, charming villages, and scenic beauty. The **town of Sirmione** is famous for its historic **Scaligero Castle**, while the surrounding mountains provide excellent hiking and cycling opportunities. Visitors can also enjoy the lake's crystal-clear waters, ideal for swimming, sailing, and windsurfing.

2.5 The Dolomites – Veneto's Mountain Wonderland

- **Location**: Northeastern Veneto, extending into **Trentino-Alto Adige**
- **Highlights**:
    - **Cortina d'Ampezzo**: A famous ski resort and part of the Dolomiti Superski area.
    - **Tre Cime di Lavaredo**: Iconic mountain peaks offering challenging hiking trails and panoramic views.
    - **Val di Zoldo**: Known for its charming villages and alpine landscapes.
    - **Alleghe**: A picturesque lake surrounded by the Dolomites, ideal for skiing and hiking.

The **Dolomites**, a UNESCO World Heritage Site, are a mountain range offering breathtaking views and a wide range of outdoor activities, from skiing and snowboarding in the winter to hiking, mountain biking, and climbing in the summer. The famous resort town of **Cortina d'Ampezzo** is a popular base for exploring the region and hosts numerous international events. For those looking to immerse themselves in nature, the Dolomites offer some of Italy's most dramatic and beautiful landscapes.

3. Cultural Highlights of Veneto

Veneto is a region steeped in art, history, and culture, offering visitors a deep dive into Italy's past.

- **Venetian Renaissance Art**: The region is home to many masterpieces by painters such as **Titian**, **Tintoretto**, and **Veronese**. These works can be found in the **Accademia Gallery** in Venice and **Museo di Castelvecchio** in Verona.
- **Architectural Landmarks**: Veneto is famous for its **Palladian Villas**, designed by architect **Andrea Palladio**, scattered throughout the region, particularly in the Vicenza area.
- **Festivals**: Veneto is home to several famous festivals, such as the **Venice Carnival** (a grand event with elaborate masks and costumes) and **Verona Opera Festival**, which takes place in the Roman **Arena di Verona**.

4. Practical Information for Visiting Veneto

- **Best Time to Visit**:

    - **Spring (April–June)**: Ideal for exploring cities, with mild weather and fewer tourists.
    - **Autumn (September–October)**: A great time for lovers, as the harvest season is in full swing, particularly in **Valpolicella** and **Prosecco** regions.
    - **Winter (December–February)**: A great time to visit the **Dolomites** for skiing or experience the festive atmosphere of **Venice Carnival**.
- **Getting Around**: Veneto has a well-developed transportation system, with excellent train services connecting the major cities. **Venice** has a unique transport network of canals, with water buses and water taxis being the primary mode of transport. Renting a car is ideal for exploring the countryside and more remote towns like **Cortina d'Ampezzo**.

Veneto is a region that offers something for everyone: the romantic canals of **Venice**, the ancient amphitheaters of **Verona**, the serene waters of **Lake Garda**, and the majestic peaks of the **Dolomites**. With its rich cultural heritage, diverse landscapes, and iconic landmarks, Veneto is one of Italy's most captivating destinations. Whether you're an art lover, an outdoor enthusiast, or a history buff, Veneto promises to be an unforgettable experience.

6.3 Emilia-Romagna

Emilia-Romagna, one of Italy's most diverse and culturally rich regions, is located in the heart of the country's northern region. Known for its gastronomic excellence, vibrant cities, historical landmarks, and beautiful countryside, Emilia-Romagna offers an exceptional blend of culture, history, and modernity. From the food capital of **Bologna** to the ancient towns of **Ravenna** and **Modena**, this region promises travelers a taste of Italy's finest traditions, both culinary and cultural.

1. Overview of Emilia-Romagna

- **Capital**: Bologna
- **Location**: Northern Italy, bordered by **Lombardy** and **Veneto** to the north, **Tuscany** to the south, **Marche** and **Liguria** to the east, and **Piedmont** to the west.
- **Area**: 22,446 square kilometers (8,662 square miles)
- **Population**: Approximately 4.5 million

- **Famous for**: Culinary heritage (Parmigiano-Reggiano, Balsamic vinegar, Prosciutto di Parma), rich history, UNESCO World Heritage Sites, and world-renowned motor racing heritage.

Emilia-Romagna is a region that thrives on both its historical significance and its contributions to Italian food culture. It is home to UNESCO sites, charming medieval towns, expansive vineyards, and some of Italy's most famous cities. Whether you're indulging in authentic pasta dishes, exploring Renaissance art, or taking in the breathtaking views of its rolling hills, Emilia-Romagna delivers a memorable experience.

2. Major Attractions in Emilia-Romagna

2.1 Bologna – The Culinary Capital

- **Location**: Central Emilia-Romagna
- **Highlights**:
    - **Piazza Maggiore**: Bologna's central square, surrounded by stunning medieval buildings and landmarks such as **Basilica di San Petronio**.
    - **Le Due Torri (The Two Towers)**: The iconic medieval towers, **Asinelli** and **Garisenda**, that dominate Bologna's skyline.
    - **Bologna's Porticoes**: Over 38 kilometers of arcades, making Bologna one of the most unique cities in Italy.
    - **Pasta Making**: Bologna is the birthplace of **tagliatelle al ragù** (commonly known as Bolognese sauce), and visitors can learn to make this iconic dish at local cooking schools.
    - **Pinacoteca Nazionale**: An art gallery showcasing works by **Giotto**, **Raffaello**, and other Italian masters.

Bologna is renowned for its gastronomic delights and is considered Italy's food capital. In addition to its famous pasta dishes, Bologna is also home to rich medieval architecture, including the **Two Towers** and the impressive **Piazza Maggiore**. The city is a vibrant mix of medieval and Renaissance history, academic tradition (it is home to the oldest university in Europe), and culinary artistry.

2.2 Modena – Land of Motors and Balsamic Vinegar

- **Location**: Northern Emilia-Romagna, near the Po River
- **Highlights**:
    - **Museo Ferrari**: A must-see for car enthusiasts, showcasing the history of the iconic Ferrari brand.

- **Modena Cathedral**: A UNESCO World Heritage Site and a prime example of Romanesque architecture.
- **Balsamic Vinegar Tour**: Visit traditional **Acetaie** (vinegar producers) to learn about and taste **Aceto Balsamico di Modena** (traditional balsamic vinegar).
- **Piazza Grande**: The city's main square, surrounded by the **Palazzo Comunale** and the **Ghirlandina Tower**.
- **Albinelli Market**: A historical market known for its local produce, including Modena's famous cured meats and cheeses.

Modena is a city known for its culinary prowess, particularly its **balsamic vinegar**, which is aged for years to develop rich flavors. The town also holds a deep connection to motorsport culture, being the birthplace of **Ferrari** and **Maserati**. With its medieval architecture and strong culinary identity, Modena attracts food lovers and car aficionados alike.

2.3 Ravenna – Mosaics and Byzantine Art

- **Location**: Eastern Emilia-Romagna, near the Adriatic Sea
- **Highlights**:
    - **Basilica di San Vitale**: A UNESCO World Heritage Site featuring stunning Byzantine mosaics.
    - **Mausoleum of Galla Placidia**: Known for its magnificent mosaic ceilings.
    - **Basilica di Sant'Apollonia in Classe**: A treasure trove of early Christian mosaics.
    - **Dante's Tomb**: The final resting place of **Dante Alighieri**, the author of **The Divine Comedy**.
    - **Ravenna's Mosaics Trail**: A self-guided tour of the city's many mosaics, showcasing the art from the Byzantine period.

Ravenna is renowned for its exceptional Byzantine mosaics, which adorn its churches and mausoleums. These ancient mosaics, which date back to the 5th and 6th centuries, make Ravenna a UNESCO World Heritage site and an important destination for art lovers. The city also holds historical significance as the capital of the Western Roman Empire during the 5th century.

2.4 Rimini – The Adriatic Coast

- **Location**: Southeastern Emilia-Romagna, along the Adriatic Sea
- **Highlights**:

- **Arch of Augustus**: A Roman monument marking the entrance to the ancient city.
- **Tempio Malatestiano**: A Renaissance church that houses works by **Piero della Francesca**.
- **Rimini Beaches**: Known for its long stretch of sandy coastline, perfect for beachgoers.
- **Italia in Miniatura**: A miniature park with replicas of Italy's most famous landmarks.
- **Fiabilandia**: A family-friendly theme park featuring rides and attractions.

Rimini is a popular seaside resort town on the Adriatic coast, offering beautiful beaches, vibrant nightlife, and a blend of ancient Roman history and modern leisure. The city's rich historical background is showcased in landmarks such as the **Arch of Augustus**, while its beaches offer a perfect escape for relaxation and water sports.

2.5 Ferrara – Renaissance Splendor

- **Location**: Northern Emilia-Romagna, along the Po River
- **Highlights**:
    - **Castello Estense**: A Renaissance castle surrounded by a moat, with a museum and stunning views of the city.
    - **Palazzo dei Diamanti**: A grand palace that houses the **Pinacoteca Nazionale**.
    - **Cattedrale di San Giorgio**: A cathedral known for its Romanesque and Gothic architecture.
    - **Renaissance Walls**: The well-preserved medieval walls of Ferrara, ideal for cycling around the city.

Ferrara is a UNESCO World Heritage city that flourished during the Renaissance period under the **Este family**. The city is known for its perfectly preserved Renaissance architecture, including the imposing **Castello Estense** and the ornate **Palazzo dei Diamanti**. Ferrara is also a great city for cycling, with extensive bike paths that take you through its historic neighborhoods.

3. Cultural Highlights of Emilia-Romagna

Emilia-Romagna is rich in culture, boasting several UNESCO World Heritage sites, historic cities, and vibrant traditions.

- **Music and Opera**: The region is known for its contributions to classical music, particularly the works of composer **Giuseppe Verdi** (born in **Busseto**) and the famous opera houses in cities like **Parma**.
- **Food and** : Emilia-Romagna is home to some of Italy's most famous foods, such as **Parmigiano-Reggiano**, **Prosciutto di Parma**, **Tortellini**, and **Balsamic Vinegar**. The region is also known for producing fine s, including **Lambrusco**, **Sangiovese**, and **Trebbiano**.
- **Motor Racing**: Emilia-Romagna is the birthplace of **Ferrari** and **Maserati**. The region's **Mugello Circuit** and **Imola Circuit** are famous for hosting international motorsport events.

4. Practical Information for Visiting Emilia-Romagna

- **Best Time to Visit**:
    - **Spring (April–June)**: Pleasant temperatures and ideal for exploring cities and countryside.
    - **Autumn (September–November)**: Perfect for food lovers, with the harvest season and food festivals like **Tortellini Festival** and **Balsamic Vinegar Week**.
    - **Summer (July–August)**: While it can be hot, the Adriatic coast offers beautiful beach vacations.
- **Getting Around**: Emilia-Romagna has an excellent transportation system, with high-speed trains connecting cities like **Bologna**, **Modena**, and **Ravenna**. Renting a car is ideal for exploring the countryside and smaller towns. The region also offers bus and tram services in most cities.

Emilia-Romagna is a treasure trove of history, culture, and culinary delights. Whether you're strolling through the medieval streets of **Bologna**, exploring the mosaics of **Ravenna**, savoring fine food in **Modena**, or relaxing on the beaches of **Rimini**, the region offers a wealth of experiences for every type of traveler. Its unique blend of cultural heritage, gastronomic excellence, and scenic beauty makes it a must-visit destination in Northern Italy.

6.4 Trentino-Alto Adige

Trentino-Alto Adige, also known as South Tyrol, is a unique and diverse region in Northern Italy. It is a place where Italian and Austrian cultures meet, creating a fascinating blend of languages, customs, and traditions. Surrounded by the majestic Alps, the region offers some of Italy's most breathtaking landscapes, including stunning mountain vistas, crystal-clear lakes, and picturesque villages. Whether you're seeking outdoor adventure, cultural experiences, or relaxation, Trentino-Alto Adige is a region that has something for everyone.

1. Overview of Trentino-Alto Adige

- **Capital**: Trento (Trentino) and Bolzano (South Tyrol)
- **Location**: Northeastern Italy, bordered by **Austria** to the north and **Switzerland** to the west, with the **Dolomites** mountain range at its core.
- **Area**: 13,607 square kilometers (5,258 square miles)
- **Population**: Approximately 1 million
- **Famous for**: Alpine beauty, outdoor activities (skiing, hiking, climbing), production, and the unique blend of Italian and Austrian cultures.

Trentino-Alto Adige is one of the most diverse and scenic regions of Italy. Its position at the crossroads of two cultures—Italian and Germanic—has shaped its rich history, architecture, and cuisine. The region is known for its outdoor offerings, from skiing in winter to hiking and cycling in the warmer months. The Dolomites, a UNESCO World Heritage Site, dominate the landscape, providing a stunning backdrop for visitors.

2. Major Attractions in Trentino-Alto Adige

2.1 Dolomites – Natural Splendor

- **Location**: Extends across Trentino-Alto Adige, Veneto, and Friuli Venezia Giulia
- **Highlights**:
    - **Alpe di Siusi**: Europe's largest high-altitude plateau, ideal for skiing in winter and hiking in summer.
    - **Lago di Braies**: A stunning emerald-green lake set against the towering peaks of the Dolomites, perfect for photography and boat trips.
    - **Sella Ronda**: A famous ski circuit that offers panoramic views of the Dolomites while skiing or snowboarding.
    - **Cortina d'Ampezzo**: A world-renowned ski resort town, known for its luxury hotels and vibrant après-ski scene.
    - **Tre Cime di Lavaredo**: One of the most iconic mountain formations in the Dolomites, offering incredible hiking trails and breathtaking views.

The **Dolomites** are the crown jewel of Trentino-Alto Adige, attracting adventure enthusiasts and nature lovers from around the world. The mountain range offers some of the best skiing and snowboarding in Europe, but it's also a summer paradise for hikers, climbers, and cyclists. The dramatic landscapes, with towering rock formations and deep valleys, make the Dolomites a must-visit destination in Northern Italy.

2.2 Bolzano – The Gateway to the Dolomites

- **Location**: Southern part of South Tyrol, near the Dolomites
- **Highlights**:
  - **Ötzi the Iceman Museum**: A museum dedicated to the discovery of **Ötzi**, the prehistoric man found frozen in the Alps, providing a glimpse into ancient life.
  - **Piazza Walther**: The main square of Bolzano, lined with cafés and shops, offering a blend of Italian and Austrian influences.
  - **Castel Roncolo**: A medieval castle featuring beautiful frescoes and panoramic views of the surrounding valley.
  - **South Tyrol Museum of Archaeology**: A museum dedicated to the region's archaeology, showcasing ancient artifacts and a deep dive into South Tyrol's history.
  - **Christmas Markets**: Bolzano is famous for its festive Christmas markets, offering a mix of local handicrafts, festive foods, and mulled .

Bolzano is the capital of South Tyrol and an essential starting point for exploring the Dolomites. With a mix of Italian and Austrian architecture, Bolzano offers a glimpse of both cultures. Its historical sites, charming town center, and proximity to the mountains make it an ideal base for exploring the surrounding natural wonders.

2.3 Trento – Historical Charm and Alpine Beauty

- **Location**: Central Trentino, at the foot of the Alps
- **Highlights**:
  - **Piazza Duomo**: A picturesque square surrounded by Renaissance buildings, including the **Trento Cathedral** and **Palazzo Pretorio**.
  - **Castello del Buonconsiglio**: A medieval castle housing the Museo Provinciale d'Arte (Provincial Art Museum) and offering stunning views of Trento and the surrounding mountains.
  - **MUSE (Museum of Science)**: A modern science museum that features interactive exhibits on nature, technology, and the environment.
  - **Monte Bondone**: A mountain ideal for hiking in the summer and skiing in the winter, with panoramic views of Trento.
  - **Palazzo delle Albere**: A historic palace that houses art exhibitions and cultural events.

Trento, the capital of Trentino, is a city rich in history, art, and culture. The city is home to impressive Renaissance architecture, including the **Trento Cathedral** and **Castello del Buonconsiglio**, as well as modern attractions like the **MUSE Science Museum**. Set against the backdrop of the Alps, Trento is the perfect blend of natural beauty and historical charm.

2.4 Lake Caldaro – Scenic Beauty

- **Location**: Southern part of South Tyrol, near Bolzano
- **Highlights**:
  - **Lago di Caldaro**: A serene, alpine lake ideal for swimming, boating, and relaxing by the water's edge.
  - **-Tasting**: The surrounding vineyards produce excellent s, particularly **Gewürztraminer** and **Sauvignon Blanc**.
  - **Castel d'Enna**: A medieval castle that offers panoramic views of Lake Caldaro and the surrounding valley.
  - **Hiking and Cycling**: Trails around the lake and through vineyards offer picturesque views of the landscape.

Lake Caldaro is a peaceful retreat that offers a mix of outdoor activities, such as swimming, hiking, and cycling. The region is also known for its excellent production, with local ries offering tastings of South Tyrol's best s. The area around the lake is perfect for a relaxing day surrounded by nature.

2.5 Merano – Wellness and Nature

- **Location**: Southern South Tyrol, near the border with Austria
- **Highlights**:
  - **Thermal Baths**: Merano is famous for its thermal spas, offering relaxing treatments in the heart of the Alps.
  - **Trauttmansdorff Castle Gardens**: A botanical garden with stunning views of Merano and the surrounding mountains, featuring themed gardens and a collection of plants from around the world.
  - **Merano's Old Town**: A charming historic center filled with boutiques, cafés, and markets.
  - **Skiing and Snowboarding**: The nearby **Schnalstal Valley** offers excellent skiing conditions in winter.
  - **Christmas Markets**: Merano's Christmas markets are particularly famous for their festive ambiance and alpine handicrafts.

Merano is a spa town famous for its wellness offerings, particularly its thermal baths that have attracted visitors for centuries. In addition to its relaxation opportunities, Merano offers cultural experiences, charming streets lined with shops and cafés, and access to stunning natural beauty, including mountains and vineyards.

3. Cultural Highlights of Trentino-Alto Adige

- **Bilingual Culture**: The region is officially bilingual, with both **Italian** and **German** spoken in South Tyrol, and a mix of both languages in Trentino. This cultural diversity is reflected in the region's cuisine, architecture, and traditions.
- **Cuisine**: The food in Trentino-Alto Adige is a blend of Italian and Austrian influences. Dishes such as **canederli** (dumplings), **speck** (smoked ham), and **strudel** are commonly found, alongside hearty mountain dishes.
- **Festivals**: The region hosts several festivals throughout the year, including the **Törggelen** harvest festival in autumn, celebrating local s and traditional dishes, and the **Merano Christmas Market**.
- **Regions**: South Tyrol is one of Italy's top -producing areas, known for its crisp white s such as **Pinot Grigio**, **Gewürztraminer**, and **Sauvignon Blanc**.

4. Practical Information for Visiting Trentino-Alto Adige

- **Best Time to Visit**:

    - **Winter (December–March)**: Ideal for skiing, snowboarding, and winter hiking in the Dolomites.
    - **Summer (June–September)**: Perfect for hiking, cycling, and exploring the lakes, gardens, and towns of the region.
    - **Autumn (September–November)**: Great for experiencing the harvest season, festivals, and cooler weather for hiking.
- **Getting Around**: The region is well connected by train and bus services, especially in the larger cities like **Bolzano**, **Trento**, and **Merano**. For more remote areas, renting a car is recommended. The area is also famous for its well-marked hiking and cycling paths.

Trentino-Alto Adige is a paradise for nature lovers, outdoor enthusiasts, and those seeking a unique cultural experience. From the majestic Dolomites to the charming towns of **Bolzano** and **Merano**, the region offers a perfect balance of relaxation, adventure, and cultural exploration. Whether you're skiing in winter, hiking in the summer, or simply enjoying the peaceful beauty of the Alps, Trentino-Alto Adige is a place where every traveler can find something special.

Chapter 7. Accommodations

7.1 Luxury Hotels and Resorts in Northern Italy

Northern Italy is home to some of the most luxurious and opulent accommodations, offering unparalleled comfort, exceptional service, and stunning views. From iconic hotels in Venice to lavish resorts along the shores of Lake Como, this region offers a variety of high-end options for discerning travelers. Below are some of the finest luxury hotels and resorts in Northern Italy, featuring distinctive designs, exquisite amenities, and a prime location in the heart of Italy's most renowned destinations.

1. The Gritti Palace – Venice

- **Price**: Starting from €800 per night
- **Address**: Campo Santa Maria del Giglio, 30124 Venezia VE, Italy
- **Contact**: +39 041 794611
- **Location**: Located on the Grand Canal, offering magnificent views of the water and the surrounding historic buildings.
- **Key Features**:
    - Classic Venetian décor with antique furniture, Murano glass chandeliers, and elegant artwork.
    - Exclusive suites with views of the Grand Canal and San Marco Basilica.

- Fine dining at **Club del Doge** restaurant, offering traditional Venetian cuisine.
- **Spa and Wellness**: Full-service spa with signature treatments, steam room, and fitness center.
- Private boat service for guest transfers to key attractions around Venice.
- **Visitor Services**:
  - Concierge service for exclusive experiences, including gondola rides, private tours of Venice's museums, and ticketing for concerts.
  - 24-hour room service and multilingual staff.
  - Access to the hotel's private art collection and guided tours of Venice.
- **Website**: www.thegrittipalace.com

The Gritti Palace is a symbol of Venetian luxury and grandeur. Situated along Venice's iconic Grand Canal, this 16th-century palace combines the elegance of Venetian heritage with modern comforts. Guests can enjoy a sophisticated atmosphere, exclusive services, and proximity to landmarks like Piazza San Marco and the Rialto Bridge.

2. Hotel Principe di Savoia – Milan

- **Price**: Starting from €500 per night
- **Address**: Piazza della Repubblica, 17, 20124 Milano MI, Italy
- **Contact**: +39 02 62301
- **Location**: Located in the heart of Milan, near the **Corso Buenos Aires** shopping district and Milan's business hub.
- **Key Features**:
  - Beautifully restored Belle Époque building with elegant interiors, featuring period décor and contemporary touches.
  - Rooftop terrace with panoramic views of Milan's skyline and the Alps.
  - **Spa and Wellness**: An award-winning spa with rejuvenating treatments, a sauna, and a swimming pool.
  - Exclusive fine dining at **Il Salotto**, serving Italian cuisine with a modern twist.
  - **Meeting and Event Facilities**: Ideal for corporate events and weddings, offering modern meeting rooms with state-of-the-art technology.
- **Visitor Services**:
  - 24-hour concierge service offering bespoke shopping experiences and access to Milan's high-fashion boutiques.
  - Private limousine transfers and helicopter services for VIP guests.

- o Pet-friendly services and family-friendly amenities available.
- **Website**: www.hotelprincipedisavoia.com

Hotel Principe di Savoia is a luxurious hotel located in Milan's prestigious city center. Known for its refined ambiance, this hotel is a blend of old-world charm and contemporary sophistication. Its central location, world-class dining, and premium services make it a top choice for both leisure and business travelers.

3. Villa d'Este – Lake Como

- **Price**: Starting from €1,200 per night
- **Address**: Via Regina 40, 22012 Cernobbio CO, Italy
- **Contact**: +39 031 3481
- **Location**: Nestled on the shores of Lake Como, just a short distance from the town of **Cernobbio** and close to the city of **Como**.
- **Key Features**:
    - o Situated within a 25-acre park with beautiful gardens and direct access to Lake Como.
    - o Exclusive lakeside villas and historic rooms with views over the water.
    - o **Spa and Wellness**: A luxurious wellness center with a full range of treatments, an indoor pool, a hot tub, and a sauna.
    - o **Dining**: Two Michelin-starred restaurants, **La Veranda** and **Il Platano**, offering gourmet Italian cuisine.
    - o Water-based activities such as private boat tours and watersports on Lake Como.
- **Visitor Services**:
    - o Private concierge service arranging bespoke activities such as helicopter tours, cooking classes, and private tastings.
    - o Butler service and personal shopping experiences for high-end clientele.
    - o Kids' club and family-friendly accommodations available.
- **Website**: www.villadeste.com

Villa d'Este is one of the most iconic luxury hotels in the world, offering a serene retreat by Lake Como. This historic property boasts exceptional service, stunning views, and opulent facilities. Guests can enjoy tranquility in one of the most picturesque locations in Northern Italy, with activities designed for relaxation and indulgence.

4. Borgo Egnazia – Puglia

- **Price**: Starting from €500 per night
- **Address**: Strada Comunale Egnazia, 72015 Savelletri di Fasano BR, Italy
- **Contact**: +39 080 225 5555

- **Location**: Located in the **Valle d'Itria** in Puglia, close to the coast and surrounded by rolling hills, the Borgo Egnazia offers an enchanting setting for relaxation.
- **Key Features**:
  - Traditional **Masseria-style** accommodation, with a mix of trulli (stone huts), private villas, and luxurious suites.
  - World-class **Vair Spa** offering tailored wellness treatments using local herbs and oils.
  - Stunning outdoor pools, and an 18-hole golf course designed by the famous architect **Dave Thomas**.
  - **Fine Dining**: Multiple restaurants offering Mediterranean dishes with local ingredients, particularly seafood, fresh pasta, and Pugliese specialties.
  - **Family-friendly**: Activities for children, including cooking classes and treasure hunts, plus childcare services.
- **Visitor Services**:
  - Exclusive transportation options such as private cars, yacht rentals, and helicopter services.
  - Personal concierge for arranging unique experiences like private dinners, tastings, and excursions.
  - Fitness center and yoga sessions available.
- **Website**: www.borgoegnazia.com

Borgo Egnazia offers a luxurious and authentic Puglian experience, with a focus on regional heritage, wellness, and extraordinary service. Set amidst ancient olive groves and rolling hills, it's perfect for travelers looking for both relaxation and adventure in a unique, peaceful setting.

5. Grand Hotel Tremezzo – Lake Como

- **Price**: Starting from €900 per night
- **Address**: Via Regina, 8, 22016 Tremezzo CO, Italy
- **Contact**: +39 0344 42491
- **Location**: Located on the western shores of **Lake Como**, offering panoramic views of the lake and the surrounding mountains.
- **Key Features**:
  - Iconic Art Nouveau architecture with grand rooms, suites, and lakeside villas.
  - **Luxury Spa**: Full-service wellness center with treatments designed to rejuvenate and relax, plus a floating pool on the lake.

- Exclusive restaurants serving refined Italian and international cuisine, including **La Terrazza** and **L'Escale**.
            - Private beach and boat service for guest excursions around Lake Como and nearby towns.
    - **Visitor Services**:
        - Personal concierge for arranging private tours, boat trips, tastings, and cooking classes.
        - Pet-friendly with designated dog services available.
        - 24-hour room service and VIP transportation services available.
    - **Website**: www.grandhoteltremezzo.com

Grand Hotel Tremezzo is an iconic hotel overlooking Lake Como, where classic elegance and contemporary luxury meet. Offering breathtaking views, five-star facilities, and an exceptional level of service, it is one of the most sought-after destinations in Northern Italy for those seeking an unforgettable stay.

These luxury hotels and resorts offer visitors not only luxurious accommodations but also a rich cultural experience, with bespoke services and access to the finest that Northern Italy has to offer. Whether on the shores of Lake Como, nestled in the mountains of Trentino, or in the heart of Milan or Venice, these properties promise unforgettable stays in one of the most beautiful regions of Europe.

7.2 Mid-Range and Boutique Hotels in Northern Italy

For travelers seeking a balance between luxury and affordability, Northern Italy boasts an array of charming mid-range and boutique hotels that provide personalized experiences, elegant accommodations, and exceptional value. These hotels offer an ideal combination of comfort, location, and unique design, often with a local flair and a focus on hospitality. Below are some of the best mid-range and boutique hotels in Northern Italy.

1. Hotel Antiche Figure – Venice

- **Price**: Starting from €160 per night
- **Address**: Santa Croce, 687, 30135 Venezia VE, Italy
- **Contact**: +39 041 5289987
- **Location**: Situated in the Santa Croce district, right on the Grand Canal, with easy access to Venice's main attractions such as Piazza San Marco, the Rialto Bridge, and the Accademia Gallery.
- **Key Features**:
    - Cozy rooms with classic Venetian furnishings and views of the Grand Canal or the peaceful internal courtyard.

- A traditional Venetian breakfast served in an elegant, canal-side room with a beautiful view.
    - Free Wi-Fi and air conditioning in all rooms.
    - Water taxis and gondola stations nearby for easy transportation to explore Venice.
- **Visitor Services**:
    - Concierge service to help with booking tickets, tours, and gondola rides.
    - 24-hour front desk and luggage storage.
    - Family-friendly, with child care available on request.
- **Website**: www.hotelantichefigure.com

Hotel Antiche Figure combines the charm of traditional Venetian hospitality with a central location, making it a perfect choice for those who want to experience the city in a comfortable yet affordable manner. Guests can enjoy scenic views of the Grand Canal from their rooms while being close to some of Venice's most iconic landmarks.

2. Hotel Artemide – Rome (Accessible for Day Trips from Northern Italy)

- **Price**: Starting from €200 per night
- **Address**: Via Nazionale, 22, 00184 Roma RM, Italy
- **Contact**: +39 06 489911
- **Location**: Ideally located near Termini Station, offering easy access to Rome's historical sites and public transport connections to Northern Italy's cities.
- **Key Features**:
    - Stylish modern rooms with elegant décor and contemporary comforts, including a wellness center and rooftop terrace with a panoramic view.
    - On-site restaurant **Ambrosia Restaurant & Bar**, offering Mediterranean cuisine with local ingredients.
    - Complimentary wellness facilities, including a fitness center, steam room, and sauna.
    - Private tour and transfer services available.
- **Visitor Services**:
    - 24-hour concierge and multilingual staff.
    - Business services, including meeting rooms and free Wi-Fi in public areas.
    - Discounts for local tours, museums, and restaurants.
- **Website**: www.hotelartemide.it

Hotel Artemide is an exceptional boutique hotel in Rome, offering a great blend of modern amenities and traditional Italian hospitality. It serves as an excellent base for exploring Rome and easily accessible for day trips to Northern Italy, such as Florence or Venice, through high-speed trains.

3. Hotel Spadari al Duomo – Milan

- **Price**: Starting from €180 per night
- **Address**: Via Spadari, 11, 20123 Milano MI, Italy
- **Contact**: +39 02 874278
- **Location**: Located in the heart of Milan, just a 5-minute walk from the iconic **Duomo Cathedral** and the **Galleria Vittorio Emanuele II**.
- **Key Features**:
  - Contemporary art and design with personalized rooms and suites, many offering views of Milan's historic center.
  - Complimentary breakfast with fresh Italian pastries, coffee, and regional delicacies.
  - In-house bar serving a selection of Italian s and local cheeses.
  - Free Wi-Fi, 24-hour room service, and air conditioning in all rooms.
- **Visitor Services**:
  - 24-hour concierge desk offering tour bookings, event tickets, and restaurant recommendations.
  - Airport transfers and private taxi services available.
  - Business corner with computer access and printing services.
- **Website**: www.hotelspadari.com

Hotel Spadari al Duomo is the ideal boutique hotel for art lovers and urban explorers visiting Milan. This hotel offers a refined setting with a modern touch, ensuring both convenience and comfort while being at the center of Milan's fashion and cultural scene.

4. Palazzo Ravizza – Siena (Tuscany Region)

- **Price**: Starting from €150 per night
- **Address**: Viale dei Mille, 24, 53100 Siena SI, Italy
- **Contact**: +39 0577 288167
- **Location**: Located just outside the historic city center of Siena, within walking distance to the famous **Piazza del Campo** and **Siena Cathedral**.
- **Key Features**:
  - Historic 18th-century building with elegant rooms featuring antique furniture, high ceilings, and original frescoes.
  - Beautiful gardens and outdoor terrace with views of the Tuscan countryside.
  - Complimentary continental breakfast with local delicacies.
  - Central location allowing easy exploration of the city's medieval landmarks.
- **Visitor Services**:

- - Complimentary Wi-Fi and parking for guests.
  - Concierge service to assist with bookings for local tours, tastings, and transportation.
  - Luggage storage and laundry services.
- **Website**: www.palazzoravizza.com

Palazzo Ravizza offers a quintessential Tuscan experience with its combination of period architecture and modern conveniences. Its proximity to Siena's historic center and peaceful atmosphere makes it an excellent base for exploring the enchanting Tuscan landscape and local vineyards.

5. NH Collection Milano President – Milan

- **Price**: Starting from €220 per night
- **Address**: Largo Augusto, 10, 20122 Milano MI, Italy
- **Contact**: +39 02 854421
- **Location**: Ideally located in Milan's city center, just steps away from the **Duomo Cathedral** and **La Scala Opera House**.
- **Key Features**:
  - Spacious and stylish rooms with a contemporary design, comfortable bedding, and modern amenities.
  - The hotel offers a **rooftop terrace** with spectacular views of Milan's skyline and the **Duomo Cathedral**.
  - On-site **restaurant** serving international and Italian dishes, with a focus on fresh, seasonal ingredients.
  - **Business facilities**: Meeting rooms, high-speed internet, and audiovisual equipment for corporate events.
- **Visitor Services**:
  - 24-hour reception and concierge services for arranging private tours, reservations, and airport transfers.
  - In-room dining, fitness center, and dry-cleaning services.
  - Pet-friendly services upon request.
- **Website**: www.nh-hotels.com

NH Collection Milano President is a perfect mix of modern elegance and Italian hospitality, ideal for both business and leisure travelers. With a central location in Milan, the hotel offers easy access to the city's main attractions, along with excellent service and premium amenities.

6. Hotel Lucrezia – Bologna

- **Price**: Starting from €130 per night

- **Address**: Via Dei Muti, 3, 40138 Bologna BO, Italy
- **Contact**: +39 051 440216
- **Location**: Situated in the **Bologna city center**, within walking distance of the **Piazza Maggiore** and the **Two Towers**.
- **Key Features**:
  - Comfortable and elegantly furnished rooms with a mix of modern and classic Italian design.
  - Complimentary breakfast with a selection of pastries, fruit, and local meats and cheeses.
  - Close proximity to Bologna's famous gastronomic districts and market areas, including the **Quadrilatero**.
  - Wi-Fi access and air conditioning in every room.
- **Visitor Services**:
  - 24-hour front desk with multilingual staff, offering assistance with tours and restaurant bookings.
  - Ticket sales for local events and attractions.
  - Airport shuttle and private transfers available.
- **Website**: www.hotellucrezia.com

Hotel Lucrezia offers a relaxed yet stylish stay in Bologna, ideal for travelers looking to immerse themselves in the culinary capital of Italy. The hotel combines comfort, value, and a perfect location to explore Bologna's rich history and food culture.

These mid-range and boutique hotels in Northern Italy provide a unique combination of comfort, style, and location, often with a personal touch and local charm that larger hotels cannot match. Whether you're visiting Venice, Milan, or Tuscany, these accommodations ensure a memorable and affordable experience without compromising on quality or service.

7.3 Budget-Friendly Hostels and Guesthouses in Northern Italy

Northern Italy is home to an excellent selection of budget-friendly hostels and guesthouses that provide affordable accommodations without sacrificing comfort or experience. Whether you're a solo traveler, a student, or looking to explore the region on a budget, these hostels and guesthouses offer great locations, excellent service, and a welcoming atmosphere. Below are some top options for budget-conscious travelers.

1. Generator Venice – Venice

- **Price**: Starting from €35 per night (for dormitory beds)

- **Address**: Fondamenta della Misericordia, 251, 30121 Venezia VE, Italy
- **Contact**: +39 041 528 9987
- **Location**: Located in the Cannaregio district, a short walk from the Grand Canal and only 15 minutes from the Rialto Bridge and Piazza San Marco.
- **Key Features**:
    - Stylish and contemporary design with both private rooms and shared dormitories.
    - On-site bar with stunning canal views, offering a relaxed space for socializing.
    - Free Wi-Fi throughout the hostel.
    - Beautiful outdoor terrace for guests to enjoy the Venetian ambiance.
- **Visitor Services**:
    - 24-hour reception with a friendly multilingual staff.
    - Luggage storage, laundry services, and towels available for rent.
    - Weekly events, such as local tours and pizza nights, to connect with other travelers.
- **Website**: www.generatorhostels.com

Generator Venice is an ideal choice for travelers looking for affordable accommodation in one of the world's most beautiful cities. With its central location, stylish facilities, and vibrant social atmosphere, it's perfect for both groups and solo travelers.

2. Ostello Bello – Milan

- **Price**: Starting from €30 per night (for dormitory beds)
- **Address**: Via Medici, 4, 20123 Milano MI, Italy
- **Contact**: +39 02 8940 3607
- **Location**: Just a 10-minute walk from Milan's **Duomo Cathedral** and **Galleria Vittorio Emanuele II**, and well-connected to public transportation.
- **Key Features**:
    - Cozy and colorful dormitories and private rooms with modern furnishings and a relaxed atmosphere.
    - Free breakfast, including a variety of local pastries and fresh fruit.
    - 24-hour open bar with complimentary tea, coffee, and snacks.
    - Spacious common areas, including a lounge with games and a music room.
- **Visitor Services**:
    - 24-hour reception with helpful staff providing recommendations for local attractions.
    - Luggage storage and free Wi-Fi throughout the property.
    - Free city maps and free walking tours available to help guests explore Milan.

- **Website**: www.ostellobello.com

Ostello Bello is perfect for travelers who want a welcoming, social atmosphere at an affordable price. The hostel's prime location, great amenities, and commitment to making guests feel at home make it one of the best budget options in Milan.

3. Combo Torino – Turin

- **Price**: Starting from €25 per night (for dormitory beds)
- **Address**: Via Luigi Cibrario, 14, 10144 Torino TO, Italy
- **Contact**: +39 011 045 8816
- **Location**: Situated in the heart of Turin, close to major attractions such as the **Mole Antonelliana**, **Piazza Castello**, and the **Egyptian Museum**.
- **Key Features**:
  - A modern, eco-friendly hostel with both private rooms and shared dormitories.
  - Spacious common areas with a kitchen for guests to prepare their own meals.
  - A stylish café/bar serving coffee and drinks, perfect for socializing.
  - Regular cultural and music events, including local art exhibitions.
- **Visitor Services**:
  - 24-hour reception and concierge services for booking tours and transportation.
  - Free Wi-Fi, laundry facilities, and bike rentals for exploring the city.
  - Luggage storage and secure lockers in the rooms.
- **Website**: www.combotorino.com

Combo Torino offers a fresh and trendy hostel experience in Turin, with a focus on sustainability and creating a community-oriented environment for its guests. It's an excellent choice for those who want to stay in a central location and enjoy a more relaxed, creative vibe.

4. A&O Hostel – Milan

- **Price**: Starting from €24 per night (for dormitory beds)
- **Address**: Viale Monza, 108, 20128 Milano MI, Italy
- **Contact**: +39 02 9475 5395
- **Location**: Located in a residential area in the eastern part of Milan, with good public transportation links to the city center and major attractions such as **Piazza del Duomo** and **Navigli District**.
- **Key Features**:

- Simple yet comfortable rooms and dorms, offering both private and shared accommodations.
- 24-hour reception and bar serving a variety of drinks and snacks.
- Spacious lounge areas and a games room for socializing and relaxing.
- Free Wi-Fi throughout the property.
- **Visitor Services**:
    - Luggage storage, ticket sales, and tour bookings available.
    - Laundry service and vending machines for snacks and drinks.
    - Group accommodations and meeting rooms for events or conferences.
- **Website**: www.aohostels.com

A&O Hostel in Milan offers an affordable and practical option for those seeking budget-friendly accommodation while being close to the city center. The hostel's laid-back atmosphere and helpful services make it a great base for exploring the Italian fashion capital.

5. Ostello di Bergamo – Bergamo

- **Price**: Starting from €20 per night (for dormitory beds)
- **Address**: Via alla Cascina, 5, 24126 Bergamo BG, Italy
- **Contact**: +39 035 265034
- **Location**: Located just a short distance from Bergamo's historic old town (Città Alta) and easily accessible from **Bergamo Airport**.
- **Key Features**:
    - A quiet and peaceful hostel set in a green area with views over Bergamo and its surrounding mountains.
    - Clean and modern rooms with private or shared accommodations.
    - Common area with a fully equipped kitchen for self-catering.
    - Shared gardens and outdoor areas to relax and enjoy the natural surroundings.
- **Visitor Services**:
    - Free Wi-Fi in public areas and in rooms.
    - Luggage storage, bike rental, and guided tours of the city available.
    - Family-friendly with services for children, such as play areas.
- **Website**: www.ostellodibergamo.com

Ostello di Bergamo offers an excellent choice for travelers on a tight budget who want to explore the charming town of Bergamo. Its peaceful environment and great facilities make it perfect for families, couples, and solo travelers alike.

6. Hostel Gallo d'Oro – Florence

- **Price**: Starting from €28 per night (for dormitory beds)
- **Address**: Via Della Scala, 43, 50123 Firenze FI, Italy
- **Contact**: +39 055 290 659
- **Location**: Located in central Florence, just a 5-minute walk from **Santa Maria Novella** train station and within walking distance to **Piazza del Duomo** and the **Uffizi Gallery**.
- **Key Features**:
    - Bright and colorful dorm rooms with air conditioning and lockers for security.
    - A spacious lounge area with sofas and a TV, perfect for socializing with other guests.
    - A communal kitchen for guests to prepare their own meals and enjoy local specialties.
    - A bar and café offering drinks and light snacks.
- **Visitor Services**:
    - 24-hour reception and free Wi-Fi.
    - Information desk for booking tickets and tours in Florence and Tuscany.
    - Laundry facilities and luggage storage.
- **Website**: www.hostelgallodoro.com

Hostel Gallo d'Oro is a popular budget-friendly option for travelers in Florence. Its prime location, warm hospitality, and vibrant atmosphere provide an affordable base to explore the Renaissance city.

These budget-friendly hostels and guesthouses in Northern Italy offer great value without compromising on quality. Whether you're traveling solo, with friends, or as part of a group, these accommodations provide a comfortable and affordable way to experience the region's rich culture, history, and landscapes.

7.4 Unique Stays – Agriturismos and Historic Villas in Northern Italy

For travelers looking for a more distinctive and immersive experience, Northern Italy offers a range of agriturismos (farm stays) and historic villas. These accommodations allow guests to connect with the region's rural charm, rich history, and breathtaking landscapes. Here are some of the top unique stays in the region, providing an authentic Italian experience.

1. Agriturismo Ca' del Bosco – Franciacorta, Lombardy

- **Price**: Starting from €100 per night (for double occupancy)

- **Address**: Via Bellavista, 1, 25030 Erbusco BS, Italy
- **Contact**: +39 030 776 0166
- **Location**: Nestled in the heart of the Franciacorta region, in the Lombardy countryside, close to Lake Iseo and just an hour's drive from Milan.
- **Key Features**:
  - Set in a beautiful vineyard, this agriturismo offers elegant rooms with panoramic views of the rolling hills and vineyards.
  - Offers tasting tours and classes where guests can sample local Franciacorta s, one of Italy's most prestigious sparkling s.
  - The farm also produces olive oil, honey, and seasonal produce.
  - Rooms feature rustic charm with contemporary amenities, and many include a private terrace or balcony.
- **Visitor Services**:
  - and olive oil tastings, cooking classes, and guided tours of the vineyards and surrounding area.
  - Bicycle rentals for exploring the countryside.
  - On-site restaurant serving locally sourced and organic dishes.
  - Free Wi-Fi, free parking, and daily housekeeping.
- **Website**: www.cadelbosco.com

Agriturismo Ca' del Bosco is a perfect retreat for lovers and those seeking a peaceful countryside experience. Its combination of luxury and nature provides an ideal place to unwind while enjoying the region's best s.

2. Villa del Balbianello – Lenno, Lake Como

- **Price**: Starting from €400 per night (for double occupancy)
- **Address**: Via Gregoriana, 6, 22016 Lenno CO, Italy
- **Contact**: +39 0344 56110
- **Location**: Located on the western shores of Lake Como, in the picturesque town of Lenno, offering stunning views of the lake and surrounding mountains.
- **Key Features**:
  - A historic villa dating back to the 18th century, renowned for its breathtaking architecture, terraced gardens, and panoramic views of Lake Como.
  - The villa has hosted famous events, including high-profile weddings and film shoots (notably in **James Bond's "Casino Royale"**).
  - Guests can book exclusive overnight stays or visit the villa as part of a private tour.
  - Beautifully preserved rooms and expansive gardens with a private boat dock for lake access.

- **Visitor Services**:
  - Private guided tours of the villa, its grounds, and its history.
  - Boat trips on Lake Como, organized directly from the villa.
  - On-site events and weddings (by arrangement).
  - Limited accommodation options for guests seeking a truly unique stay.
- **Website**: www.fondoambiente.it

Villa del Balbianello is one of the most iconic historic villas on Lake Como, offering an exclusive and luxurious stay in a location steeped in history and natural beauty. A visit here is perfect for those looking to indulge in a high-end experience amidst an extraordinary setting.

3. Agriturismo La Costa – Monzambano, Lombardy

- **Price**: Starting from €80 per night (for double occupancy)
- **Address**: Via Costa, 13, 46040 Monzambano MN, Italy
- **Contact**: +39 0376 809160
- **Location**: Situated in the tranquil countryside of Lombardy, near the shores of Lake Garda, and within easy reach of the historic towns of **Sirmione** and **Peschiera del Garda**

.

- **Key Features**:
  - A family-run agriturismo surrounded by olive groves and vineyards, offering cozy, rustic rooms with a country-style décor.
  - Guests can enjoy on-site tasting and tours of the farm, which produces its own and olive oil.
  - A small outdoor swimming pool, garden areas, and a sun terrace where guests can relax.
  - An on-site restaurant serving traditional Lombard dishes made with fresh, local ingredients.
- **Visitor Services**:
  - and olive oil tastings and direct sales of their products.
  - Bicycle rentals to explore the beautiful countryside and nearby lakeside paths.
  - Cooking classes focused on local specialties.
  - Free Wi-Fi, free parking, and a continental breakfast included.
- **Website**: www.agriturismolacosta.it

Agriturismo La Costa is a wonderful choice for travelers seeking a quiet, authentic farm experience with the added bonus of delicious regional cuisine and . It's ideal for couples and families looking to enjoy the beauty of Lake Garda from a more relaxed, rustic perspective.

4. Villa La Massa – Florence (Tuscany)

- **Price**: Starting from €350 per night (for double occupancy)
- **Address**: Via della Massa, 24, 50012 Candeli FI, Italy
- **Contact**: +39 055 626 11
- **Location**: Located in the Tuscan hills, just a short drive from the city center of Florence, offering a luxurious and peaceful setting surrounded by olive groves and vineyards.
- **Key Features**:
  - A stunning Renaissance villa with opulent rooms, each uniquely decorated with antique furnishings and offering panoramic views of the Arno River and Tuscan countryside.
  - The villa has an on-site Michelin-starred restaurant and offers personalized cooking experiences.
  - A large outdoor pool with views over the surrounding olive groves, along with a wellness center offering spa treatments.
  - Beautifully landscaped gardens perfect for peaceful walks.

- **Visitor Services**:
  - Private cooking classes, tastings, and guided tours of Florence.
  - Full-service spa, wellness treatments, and yoga sessions.
  - Concierge services, laundry, and valet parking.
  - Free Wi-Fi and a range of luxury amenities, including private boat trips on the Arno.
- **Website**: www.villalamassa.com

Villa La Massa combines the grandeur of a historic villa with the comforts of modern luxury, providing a retreat for travelers looking to indulge in the beauty of Tuscany and Florence. Whether you want to relax by the pool, savor fine dining, or explore the artistic heart of Italy, this villa offers an unforgettable experience.

5. Agriturismo Il Rigo – Tuscany

- **Price**: Starting from €90 per night (for double occupancy)
- **Address**: Località Il Rigo, 53041, Asciano SI, Italy
- **Contact**: +39 0577 590 642

- **Location**: Located in the rolling hills of the **Crete Senesi** region in southern Tuscany, this agriturismo offers a tranquil setting just outside of the town of **Asciano** and 25 minutes from **Siena**.
- **Key Features**:
  - A charming farmhouse offering a variety of rustic rooms and apartments, some with kitchens for self-catering.
  - The farm produces its own organic , olive oil, and vegetables.
  - Guests can enjoy outdoor activities such as hiking, cycling, and birdwatching in the surrounding countryside.
  - A rustic kitchen serving traditional Tuscan dishes, prepared using ingredients grown on the property.
- **Visitor Services**:
  - and olive oil tastings, cooking classes, and organic farm tours.
  - On-site pool, yoga sessions, and bike rentals for exploring the picturesque landscapes.
  - Family-friendly, with kid-friendly activities and educational farm experiences.
  - Free Wi-Fi, parking, and a lovely garden for relaxation.
- **Website**: www.ilrigo.com

Agriturismo Il Rigo offers a fantastic opportunity to experience authentic rural Tuscany, with its stunning landscape, organic produce, and genuine hospitality. It's an excellent choice for those seeking peace and quiet while still being close to Tuscany's major historical cities.

These agriturismos and historic villas in Northern Italy provide travelers with the opportunity to experience the region in a way that combines luxury, history, and nature. Whether you are staying in the countryside, by the lakes, or in a historic villa, these unique stays offer memorable experiences that immerse you in the true Italian lifestyle.

Chapter 8. Food and Drink

8.1 Must-Try Dishes and Local Specialties in Northern Italy

Northern Italy's cuisine is a delightful fusion of rich, hearty flavors, seasonal ingredients, and culinary traditions passed down through generations. The food reflects the diverse regions, with each area offering its own distinct dishes and ingredients. From creamy risottos to rich meats, fine cheeses, and delectable desserts, here are some of the must-try dishes and local specialties when visiting Northern Italy.

1. Risotto alla Milanese (Lombardy)

- **Description**: A creamy, flavorful risotto made with Arborio rice, cooked in a rich broth and infused with saffron, which gives it a vibrant golden color and distinctive aroma.
- **Where to Try**: Milan, particularly in traditional trattorias and fine dining restaurants.
- **Pairing**: Best enjoyed with a glass of dry white from Lombardy, such as **Franciacorta** sparkling .
- **Why It's Special**: Known as a Milanese classic, it's a dish that epitomizes the city's rich culinary tradition, combining simplicity with luxury (saffron being one of the most expensive spices in the world).

2. Pizzoccheri (Lombardy/Valtellina)

- **Description**: A type of buckwheat pasta, traditionally served with a hearty mix of potatoes, cabbage, and melted cheese, often made with **bitto cheese** and garlic-infused butter.
- **Where to Try**: Valtellina region (near Sondrio), in family-run mountain restaurants.
- **Pairing**: A robust red like **Sforzato di Valtellina** works well with this comforting dish.
- **Why It's Special**: A warm and filling dish perfect for the cold mountain climate, it has been a staple of the Alpine valleys for centuries.

3. Tortellini (Emilia-Romagna)

- **Description**: Small, ring-shaped pasta stuffed with a filling of pork, beef, and cheese, traditionally served in a rich broth or with a cream sauce.
- **Where to Try**: Bologna and Modena, where **tortellini** is considered a culinary treasure.
- **Pairing**: Often paired with **Lambrusco** (a sparkling red) or a glass of **Trebbiano** white .
- **Why It's Special**: Tortellini is a beloved regional dish, known for its distinctive shape and delicate flavor, often referred to as **"the belly button of Bologna."**

4. Fondue and Polenta (Trentino-Alto Adige)

- **Description**: A delicious combination of melted cheese (usually **Fontina** or a mix of cheeses) served with **polenta** (cornmeal) and various cured meats, perfect for dipping.
- **Where to Try**: In the Dolomites region and throughout the Alpine towns of Trentino-Alto Adige.
- **Pairing**: Ideal with a glass of full-bodied red like **Lagrein** or **Schiava**.
- **Why It's Special**: The mix of hearty, warming flavors, and the rustic nature of the dish make it perfect for the alpine landscape, where it's often enjoyed as a communal meal.

5. Osso Buco (Lombardy)

- **Description**: A tender veal shank braised in white , broth, and a medley of vegetables, typically served with **gremolata** (a fresh lemon and herb condiment).
- **Where to Try**: Milan, especially in trattorias or restaurants serving traditional Lombardian cuisine.
- **Pairing**: Pairs wonderfully with a glass of **Barolo**, a rich red from the Piedmont region.

- **Why It's Special**: **Osso Buco** is a Milanese classic, often served with a side of **risotto alla Milanese** for the ultimate indulgence.

6. Polenta e Osei (Lombardy/Valtellina)

- **Description**: A traditional dessert from the Valtellina region made of sweetened **polenta** (cornmeal) served with a mix of local wild berries and **grappa**.
- **Where to Try**: Valtellina region and Lombardy.
- **Pairing**: Best with a glass of **Grappa** or a sweet dessert from the region.
- **Why It's Special**: The dessert is a great example of how Northern Italian cuisine combines the rustic simplicity of its ingredients with a touch of regional flair.

7. Bagna Cauda (Piedmont)

- **Description**: A warm dip made from anchovies, garlic, butter, and olive oil, served with a variety of raw or cooked vegetables for dipping.
- **Where to Try**: Piedmont, especially in the Langhe region, famous for its and cuisine.
- **Pairing**: Pairs beautifully with a glass of **Barbaresco** or **Barolo** from Piedmont.
- **Why It's Special**: **Bagna Cauda** is a traditional Piedmontese dish often served during the winter months, especially as part of a convivial feast with friends and family.

8. Frittelle di Riso (Veneto)

- **Description**: Rice fritters made with cooked rice, eggs, sugar, and flavored with lemon zest or cinnamon, fried to golden perfection.
- **Where to Try**: Venice and other Venetian towns, especially during the Carnival period.
- **Pairing**: A sweet such as **Prosecco** or **Vin Santo** complements the flavors of the dessert.
- **Why It's Special**: These fritters are a Carnival-time treat, but they can be found year-round in Venice and throughout the Veneto region, providing a sweet, satisfying snack.

9. Ragu alla Bolognese (Emilia-Romagna)

- **Description**: A rich, slow-cooked meat sauce made with beef, pork, tomatoes, onions, and carrots, served with pasta (typically **tagliatelle** or **tortellini**).
- **Where to Try**: Bologna, often referred to as the home of **ragù**.

- **Pairing**: This hearty dish pairs excellently with a glass of red like **Sangiovese** or **Chianti**.
- **Why It's Special**: Bologna's **ragù alla Bolognese** is one of Italy's most iconic pasta sauces, and every family has their own variation, making it a truly cherished dish in the region.

10. Gelato (All Regions)

- **Description**: Italy's famous ice cream, known for its creamy texture and intense flavor, made with fresh ingredients like fruit, nuts, chocolate, and vanilla.
- **Where to Try**: Across Northern Italy, especially in Milan, Florence, and Venice.
- **Pairing**: A refreshing lemon sorbetto works well after a heavy meal or in warm weather.
- **Why It's Special**: While **gelato** can be found all over Italy, Northern Italy's gelato stands out for using fresh, high-quality ingredients like local fruits, nuts, and chocolate.

Northern Italy's culinary offerings are diverse and deeply tied to the region's geography, history, and climate. Whether you are indulging in the rich flavors of Milanese risotto, the hearty comfort of **polenta**, or the decadent sweetness of **gelato**, these dishes are not only about food—they are about experiencing the heart and soul of Northern Italy's cultural and regional identity.

8.2 Regions of Northern Italy

Northern Italy is home to some of the country's most celebrated and diverse regions, offering a wide array of s that cater to different palates. From sparkling s to bold reds and delicate whites, the northern regions benefit from varied climates and terrains, producing s with distinct characteristics. Here's a closer look at the most notable regions in Northern Italy:

1. Piedmont

- **Key s**: **Barolo, Barbaresco, Dolcetto, Moscato d'Asti**
- **Location**: Located in the northwest, Piedmont is bordered by the Alps to the north, offering a cooler climate ideal for cultivating high-quality s.
- **Description**: Known for its prestigious reds, Piedmont is perhaps best known for its **Barolo**, often referred to as the "King of s." Made from the **Nebbiolo** grape, Barolo is full-bodied, tannic, and rich, with complex flavors that improve with age. **Barbaresco**, another Nebbiolo-based , is lighter but equally revered. In contrast, the **Moscato d'Asti** is a sweet, sparkling white that pairs beautifully with desserts. **Dolcetto**, another red variety, is fruity and approachable.

- **Top Vineyards and ries**:
    - **Gaja ry** (Barbaresco)
    - **Marchesi di Barolo** (Barolo)
    - **Cascina Bruni** (Moscato d'Asti)
- **Best Time to Visit**: September to October for the grape harvest season.

2. Veneto

- **Key s: Prosecco, Amarone della Valpolicella, Soave, Valpolicella**
- **Location**: Situated in the northeastern part of Italy, Veneto is renowned for its diverse offerings, ranging from sparkling s to full-bodied reds.
- **Description**: Veneto's most famous is **Prosecco**, a light and refreshing sparkling made from the **Glera** grape. The **Prosecco** region, particularly around **Conegliano** and **Valdobbiadene**, is a UNESCO World Heritage site, and Prosecco has become a global symbol of Italian sparkling. Veneto is also home to **Amarone della Valpolicella**, a robust, full-bodied red made from dried grapes. **Soave** is a delicate white, known for its floral aromas and crisp acidity, made primarily from the **Garganega** grape.
- **Top Vineyards and ries**:
    - **Ca' del Bosco** (Prosecco)
    - **Allegrini** (Amarone della Valpolicella)
    - **Pieropan** (Soave)
- **Best Time to Visit**: April to June for pleasant weather or during the harvest season in September.

3. Trentino-Alto Adige

- **Key s: Pinot Grigio, Lagrein, Gewürztraminer, Schiava**
- **Location**: This region is located in the northeastern corner of Italy, bordered by Austria and Switzerland. Its cool climate and mountainous landscape make it ideal for producing aromatic white s and unique reds.
- **Description**: Trentino-Alto Adige is known for its high-altitude vineyards, which produce crisp, fresh **Pinot Grigio** and **Gewürztraminer**, both of which have gained international acclaim. The region is also home to **Lagrein**, a rich red with flavors of dark fruits and spices, and **Schiava**, a lighter red that is often described as fruity and easy-drinking.
- **Top Vineyards and ries**:
    - **Cantina Tramin** (Gewürztraminer)
    - **Terlan ry** (Pinot Grigio)
    - **Kellerei Bozen** (Lagrein)
- **Best Time to Visit**: September to October for the harvest season.

4. Friuli Venezia Giulia

- **Key s**: **Friulano, Pinot Grigio, Sauvignon Blanc, Merlot**
- **Location**: Located in the far northeastern part of Italy, Friuli Venezia Giulia borders Slovenia and Austria. The region's diverse climate, ranging from the Alps to the Adriatic Sea, allows for a variety of styles.
- **Description**: Friuli Venezia Giulia is famous for its white s, particularly **Friulano**, a fresh, crisp with almond and herbal notes. **Pinot Grigio** from this region is also highly regarded for its clean, mineral-driven character. The area produces top-tier **Sauvignon Blanc** and **Merlot** as well. The region's unique terroir and mix of influences from neighboring countries contribute to the complexity of its s.
- **Top Vineyards and ries**:
    - **Livio Felluga** (Friulano)
    - **Jermann** (Pinot Grigio)
    - **Ronco del Gnemiz** (Sauvignon Blanc)
- **Best Time to Visit**: April to June for mild weather or September during the harvest.

5. Lombardy

- **Key s: Franciacorta, Valtellina Superiore, Oltrepò Pavese**
- **Location**: Lombardy, located in the northern center of Italy, is a region of great diversity, with a range of microclimates perfect for production.
- **Description: Franciacorta** is a standout sparkling made using the traditional method, similar to Champagne, and is produced in the region of **Franciacorta** in Brescia. It's known for its rich, complex flavor profile, with notes of brioche and almond. The **Valtellina Superiore** is a red made from the **Nebbiolo** grape, with flavors of cherry and spices. **Oltrepò Pavese** is known for its white s, particularly **Pinot Noir** and **Pinot Grigio**, and its sparkling **Moscato**.
- **Top Vineyards and ries**:
    - **Ca' del Bosco** (Franciacorta)
    - **Nino Negri** (Valtellina Superiore)
    - **Cascina Montalbano** (Oltrepò Pavese)
- **Best Time to Visit**: April to October for beautiful vineyard landscapes and the harvest.

6. Liguria

- **Key s: Rossese di Dolceacqua, Vermentino, Pigato**
- **Location**: Liguria is a coastal region in northwestern Italy, known for its rugged terrain and proximity to the Mediterranean Sea.

- **Description**: Liguria's regions produce distinctive s influenced by the sea and steep hillside vineyards. **Rossese di Dolceacqua** is a red that is light, aromatic, and fruity, with flavors of red berries and herbs. **Vermentino**, a white , is crisp and refreshing with citrusy notes, while **Pigato** is another white variety, full-bodied with aromas of herbs and flowers.
- **Top Vineyards and ries**:
    - **Cantina Terre Bianche** (Rossese di Dolceacqua)
    - **La Scolca** (Vermentino)
    - **Podere Ruggeri Corsini** (Pigato)
- **Best Time to Visit**: April to September for the warm Mediterranean climate and harvest season.

Northern Italy's regions offer a remarkable diversity of s, each with its own unique character, influenced by the terroir, climate, and traditions of the area. Whether you're savoring a sparkling glass of **Franciacorta** in Lombardy, indulging in a glass of rich **Barolo** in Piedmont, or enjoying a refreshing **Pinot Grigio** in Trentino-Alto Adige, the s of Northern Italy will add a rich layer to your travel experience. Be sure to explore the local vineyards, attend tastings, and enjoy the beauty of the regions while sipping their world-class s.

8.3 Best Restaurants and Cafes in Northern Italy

Northern Italy is a paradise for food lovers, offering a wide range of exceptional dining experiences. From Michelin-starred fine dining to cozy local cafés, the culinary scene is as diverse as the regions themselves. Whether you're craving classic Italian fare or innovative modern cuisine, here's a guide to some of the best restaurants and cafés across Northern Italy.

1. Osteria Francescana (Modena, Emilia-Romagna)

- **Cuisine**: Modern Italian, Fusion
- **Price**: €300-€400 per person (tasting menu)
- **Location**: Via Stella, 22, 41121 Modena MO, Italy
- **Contact**: +39 059 210118
- **Website**: osteriafrancescana.it
- **Key Features**: Three Michelin stars, innovative tasting menus, renowned chef Massimo Bottura.
- **Description**: Osteria Francescana is one of the most celebrated restaurants in the world. Led by **Massimo Bottura**, this three-Michelin-starred restaurant combines traditional Italian flavors with contemporary techniques and global influences. Dishes are playful, yet refined, making each course a work of art.

Famous dishes include "Oops! I Dropped the Lemon Tart," a creative deconstruction of the classic dessert.
- **Visitor Services**: Reservation is essential, and the restaurant also offers pairings with each course.

2. Le Calandre (Rubano, Veneto)

- **Cuisine**: Contemporary Italian
- **Price**: €220-€300 per person (tasting menu)
- **Location**: Via Liguria, 1, 35030 Rubano PD, Italy
- **Contact**: +39 049 630303
- **Website**: lecalandre.com
- **Key Features**: Three Michelin stars, elegant ambiance, culinary innovation.
- **Description**: Renowned for its imaginative approach to Italian cuisine, **Le Calandre** offers a luxurious experience with modern and seasonal ingredients. The restaurant, helmed by the **Alajmo brothers**, delivers beautifully crafted tasting menus that merge traditional Italian dishes with avant-garde techniques. Expect dishes that challenge the boundaries of flavor and texture, presented in an elegant, minimalist setting.
- **Visitor Services**: Extensive list, and a stylish dining room with impeccable service. Reservations required well in advance.

3. Da Vittorio (Brusaporto, Lombardy)

- **Cuisine**: Italian, Traditional Lombard
- **Price**: €150-€250 per person (tasting menu)
- **Location**: Via Cantalupa, 17, 24060 Brusaporto BG, Italy
- **Contact**: +39 035 681 024
- **Website**: davittorio.com
- **Key Features**: Three Michelin stars, family-run, traditional flavors with modern techniques.
- **Description**: **Da Vittorio** is a luxurious family-run restaurant that blends traditional Lombard flavors with modern techniques. The restaurant has earned three Michelin stars for its exquisite and meticulous approach to classic Italian dishes. Known for its pasta dishes, seafood, and rich meat courses, **Da Vittorio** is a celebration of northern Italian gastronomy.
- **Visitor Services**: In addition to the restaurant, the venue has an elegant cellar and offers a curated pairing experience with each meal.

4. Antica Osteria Cera (Cavallino-Treporti, Veneto)

- **Cuisine**: Seafood, Venetian

- **Price**: €100-€150 per person
- **Location**: Via Cà Ballarin, 1, 30013 Cavallino-Treporti VE, Italy
- **Contact**: +39 041 530 1152
- **Website**: anticosteriacera.com
- **Key Features**: Two Michelin stars, seafood-focused, cozy atmosphere.
- **Description**: **Antica Osteria Cera** is a Michelin-starred restaurant located on the outskirts of Venice, specializing in fresh seafood and Venetian cuisine. With a focus on high-quality, local ingredients, the restaurant creates refined, yet approachable dishes that highlight the flavors of the Adriatic coast. The intimate atmosphere and excellent service make for a memorable dining experience.
- **Visitor Services**: pairings are available, with a focus on regional Italian s, and the restaurant offers both à la carte and tasting menu options.

5. Ristorante Il Luogo di Aimo e Nadia (Milan, Lombardy)

- **Cuisine**: Italian, Contemporary
- **Price**: €180-€250 per person (tasting menu)
- **Location**: Via Montecuccoli, 6, 20147 Milan MI, Italy
- **Contact**: +39 02 416186
- **Website**: aimoenadia.com
- **Key Features**: Two Michelin stars, innovative Italian cuisine, elegant setting.
- **Description**: Located in the heart of Milan, **Il Luogo di Aimo e Nadia** is a fine-dining institution that fuses tradition with creativity. The restaurant, which has earned two Michelin stars, is known for its stunning presentations and innovative takes on classic Italian dishes. Expect fresh, seasonal ingredients transformed into works of culinary art by talented chefs **Aimo and Nadia**.
- **Visitor Services**: The restaurant offers an extensive list, and advanced reservations are highly recommended.

6. Caffè Florian (Venice, Veneto)

- **Cuisine**: Italian Café, Light Meals, Pastries
- **Price**: €15-€50 per person (depending on the order)
- **Location**: Piazza San Marco, 57, 30124 Venice VE, Italy
- **Contact**: +39 041 528 9988
- **Website**: caffeflorian.com
- **Key Features**: Historic café, luxurious setting, famous for coffee and pastries.

- **Description**: Established in 1720, **Caffè Florian** is one of the oldest and most famous cafés in Europe. Located in the iconic **Piazza San Marco**, this historic café is the perfect place to relax with a coffee while soaking in the atmosphere of Venice. It is renowned for its beautiful interior, a mix of opulent Venetian style, and exquisite pastries, including the classic **frittelle** (Venetian rice fritters) and various Italian cakes.
- **Visitor Services**: Outdoor seating with views of the square, live music performances in the evenings, and a selection of high-end coffees and teas.

7. Caffè Motta (Verona, Veneto)

- **Cuisine**: Italian Café, Light Meals, Desserts
- **Price**: €10-€30 per person
- **Location**: Piazza delle Erbe, 23, 37121 Verona VR, Italy
- **Contact**: +39 045 801 0697
- **Website**: cafemotta.com
- **Key Features**: Classic Venetian café, historic ambiance, delicious coffee and pastries.
- **Description**: **Caffè Motta** is a charming café in the heart of Verona's historic center, offering an ideal spot to unwind while exploring the city. With its beautiful Art Deco interior, **Caffè Motta** serves a wide selection of coffees, pastries, and light snacks. The café is famous for its freshly brewed espresso, delicious **cappuccino**, and homemade cakes, making it a favorite among locals and visitors alike.
- **Visitor Services**: Outdoor seating, excellent customer service, and a cozy atmosphere for a peaceful coffee break.

8. Pasticceria Marchesi (Milan, Lombardy)

- **Cuisine**: Italian Pastries, Gelato
- **Price**: €5-€25 per person
- **Location**: Via Monte Napoleone, 9, 20121 Milan MI, Italy
- **Contact**: +39 02 7600 6452
- **Website**: pasticceriamarchesi.com
- **Key Features**: Historic pastry shop, luxury pastries, elegant café setting.
- **Description**: **Pasticceria Marchesi** is a historic Milanese pastry shop and café, renowned for its high-end pastries and sophisticated setting. The beautiful store offers a range of delicacies, from freshly baked **cannoli** to delicate **millefoglie** (layered pastry). The café is a great place to enjoy a coffee while sampling some of Milan's best pastries.
- **Visitor Services**: Indoor and outdoor seating, gift packaging for pastries, and an exclusive selection of Italian sweets.

Northern Italy offers a broad spectrum of dining experiences, from elegant Michelin-starred restaurants to charming cafés steeped in history. Whether you're looking to indulge in a world-class dining experience at **Osteria Francescana**, enjoy a laid-back coffee at **Caffè Florian**, or savor a simple yet delightful meal at a traditional trattoria, Northern Italy has something for every palate. Make sure to sample the region's regional specialties and enjoy the impeccable hospitality and vibrant food culture that defines this extraordinary part of the world.

Chapter 9. Itineraries

9.1 A 7-Day Classic Northern Italy Tour

Northern Italy is a treasure trove of rich history, stunning landscapes, and world-renowned art and cuisine. This 7-day itinerary will take you through some of the region's most iconic cities and natural wonders, offering a balanced mix of culture, adventure, and relaxation.

Day 1: Arrival in Milan

- **Morning**: Arrive in **Milan**, Italy's fashion capital. Depending on your arrival time, take a leisurely walk around the city center to start soaking in the sights.
- **Afternoon**: Visit **the Duomo di Milano**, one of the most iconic Gothic cathedrals in the world. Climb to the rooftop for panoramic views of the city and the Alps in the distance.
    - **Address**: Piazza del Duomo, 20122 Milan MI, Italy
    - **Opening Hours**: 8:00 AM – 7:00 PM
    - **Ticket Price**: €15 (Cathedral), €20-€30 (Rooftop)
- **Evening**: Explore the fashionable **Galleria Vittorio Emanuele II** and have dinner at one of the city's renowned restaurants, such as **Osteria dell'Acquabella**, offering traditional Milanese dishes.

Day 2: Milan – Explore Art and Fashion

- **Morning**: Visit the **Sforza Castle** and its museums, including the **Pinacoteca** with works by artists such as Leonardo da Vinci and Michelangelo.
    - **Address**: Piazza Castello, 20121 Milan MI, Italy
    - **Opening Hours**: 7:00 AM – 9:00 PM
    - **Ticket Price**: €10-€15
- **Afternoon**: Head to **Pinacoteca di Brera**, which houses a fine collection of Italian Renaissance and Baroque masterpieces.
    - **Address**: Via Brera, 28, 20121 Milan MI, Italy
    - **Opening Hours**: 8:30 AM – 7:30 PM
    - **Ticket Price**: €15
- **Evening**: Shop in the **Quadrilatero della Moda** (Milan's luxury shopping district) or relax at a café with an aperitivo in the lively **Navigli District**.

Day 3: Milan to Venice

- **Morning**: Take a **train** or **private transfer** to **Venice** (approx. 2.5 hours).

- **Afternoon**: Once in Venice, explore **Piazza San Marco** and visit **St. Mark's Basilica**, famous for its mosaics and stunning architecture.
    - **Address**: Piazza San Marco, 30124 Venice VE, Italy
    - **Opening Hours**: 9:45 AM – 5:00 PM
    - **Ticket Price**: €5 (entry to the basilica), €20 for the museum and Pala d'Oro.
- **Evening**: Take a **Gondola Ride** through the canals or explore the quaint streets around **Rialto Bridge** and enjoy a Venetian seafood dinner at **Antiche Carampane**.

Day 4: Venice – Explore Hidden Gems

- **Morning**: Visit the **Doge's Palace** and the **Bridge of Sighs**. Learn about Venice's political history and enjoy views of the Grand Canal from the palace.
    - **Address**: Piazza San Marco, 1, 30124 Venice VE, Italy
    - **Opening Hours**: 8:30 AM – 7:00 PM
    - **Ticket Price**: €20-€25
- **Afternoon**: Wander the **Castello** district and visit **Arsenale di Venezia**, once the heart of Venice's naval power.
- **Evening**: Have dinner at **Ristorante Antico Martini**, an elegant dining spot near **La Fenice Theatre**.

Day 5: Venice to Florence

- **Morning**: Depart for **Florence** (approx. 2 hours by train).
- **Afternoon**: Visit the **Duomo** and **Baptistery of St. John**. Climb to the top of **Florence Cathedral** for incredible views of the Tuscan landscape.
    - **Address**: Piazza del Duomo, 50122 Florence FI, Italy
    - **Opening Hours**: 10:00 AM – 5:00 PM
    - **Ticket Price**: €18 (for combined tickets)
- **Evening**: Explore **Piazza della Signoria**, where you'll find **Palazzo Vecchio** and **Michelangelo's David** at the **Accademia Gallery**.
    - **Ticket Price**: €12
    - **Opening Hours**: 8:15 AM – 6:50 PM

Day 6: Florence – Explore the Renaissance Heart

- **Morning**: Visit the **Uffizi Gallery**, home to masterpieces by Botticelli, Da Vinci, and Michelangelo.
    - **Address**: Piazzale degli Uffizi, 6, 50122 Florence FI, Italy
    - **Opening Hours**: 8:15 AM – 6:50 PM
    - **Ticket Price**: €20

- **Afternoon**: Visit **Ponte Vecchio**, a medieval bridge lined with jewelry shops, and take a stroll through the **Boboli Gardens** behind **Pitti Palace** for a relaxing afternoon.
    - **Ticket Price**: €10-€15
- **Evening**: Indulge in a Tuscan dinner at **Osteria All'Antico Vinaio**, known for its fantastic **schiacciata** (Tuscan flatbread sandwiches).

Day 7: Florence to Lake Como

- **Morning**: Take a train or private transfer to **Lake Como** (approx. 4 hours by train).
- **Afternoon**: Upon arrival, explore **Bellagio**, a picturesque town located on a promontory between two branches of Lake Como. Enjoy a boat ride on the lake to admire the beautiful villas and mountains surrounding it.
    - **Key Attraction**: Visit **Villa del Balbianello**, one of the most famous villas in the region, known for its stunning gardens and views.
    - **Ticket Price**: €10-€15 for Villa tours.
- **Evening**: Enjoy a relaxing dinner with lakeside views at **Ristorante Mistral** in **Lecco** or **Cernobbio**.

Additional Tips

- **Transportation**: Trains are the most efficient way to get around Northern Italy. Book tickets in advance via the **Trenitalia** website or mobile app.
- **Weather**: Northern Italy has a Mediterranean climate. Summers can be hot, especially in cities like Florence and Milan, so pack accordingly. The best months to visit are from April to October.
- **Reservations**: Many popular attractions require advance booking, especially in Venice and Florence, so make sure to secure tickets for museums, galleries, and iconic sites.

This 7-day itinerary gives you a taste of Northern Italy's rich cultural heritage, iconic landmarks, and stunning landscapes. Whether you're in Milan for fashion, Venice for romance, or Florence for Renaissance art, this tour will immerse you in the best the region has to offer.

9.2 A 10-Day Culinary Adventure in Northern Italy

Northern Italy is a paradise for food lovers, offering a rich culinary tradition influenced by both the Mediterranean and Alpine regions. This 10-day culinary tour will take you through some of the best gastronomic destinations, from fresh pasta and truffles to world-class s and cheeses. Explore Italy's food culture through hands-on experiences, cooking classes, and visits to local markets. Let's dive into a true culinary adventure.

Day 1: Arrival in Milan – The Gateway to Lombardy's Flavors

- **Morning**: Arrive in **Milan**. After settling in, head to the **Mercato Centrale Milano**, a vibrant food market, where you can sample regional specialties, such as **risotto alla Milanese** (a saffron-infused dish) and **panettone**, a famous Milanese Christmas dessert.
    - **Address**: Via F. Sforza, 23, 20121 Milan MI, Italy
- **Afternoon**: Visit **Eataly Milan**, an upscale food emporium offering a range of local products. Participate in a **cheese-tasting session**, where you'll savor Lombardy's finest cheeses, including **Gorgonzola** and **Taleggio**.
    - **Address**: Piazza XXV Aprile, 10, 20121 Milan MI, Italy
- **Evening**: Dinner at **Osteria del Binari**, known for its **osso buco**, a Milanese specialty made with braised veal shanks.

Day 2: Milan – Pasta and Risotto

- **Morning**: Visit a traditional **pasta workshop** to learn how to make Milanese-style **pasta** from scratch. Follow the chef's guidance in preparing delicate dishes like **pasta alla Milanese**.
- **Afternoon**: Enjoy a hands-on cooking class that focuses on the classic **risotto alla Milanese**, learning how to infuse the dish with saffron and create the perfect creamy texture.
- **Evening**: Dine at **Trattoria Milanese**, where you can try a traditional Milanese **risotto**, paired with a glass of **Nebbiolo** from the Piedmont region.

Day 3: Milan to Piedmont – Truffle Country

- **Morning**: Take a train or private transfer to **Alba**, the heart of **Piedmont**, renowned for its **white truffles**. Visit a local truffle market or attend a **truffle-hunting tour** led by an expert truffle hunter and trained dogs.
- **Afternoon**: Visit a ry in the **Langhe region**, home to some of the best s in the world, such as **Barolo** and **Barbaresco**. Take a tour and enjoy a -tasting session.
    - **Key Vineyard**: **Marchesi di Barolo ry**
    - **Address**: Via Roma, 1, 12060 Barolo CN, Italy
    - **Ticket Price**: €25-€50 for a guided tour with tasting.
- **Evening**: Dinner at a local restaurant in Alba, where you can indulge in **tajarin pasta** topped with freshly grated white truffles and paired with Barolo .

Day 4: Piedmont – The Heart of Fine s and Hazelnuts

- **Morning**: Visit a **hazelnut farm** in the Langhe region, where you'll learn about the prized **Tonda Gentile** hazelnut variety. Taste hazelnut products such as spreads, pralines, and cakes.
- **Afternoon**: Visit **La Morra**, a hilltop town famous for its estates. Enjoy a **Barolo -tasting session** with local cheeses and meats.
- **Evening**: Dine at **Ristorante Bovio**, which offers a modern take on traditional Piedmontese dishes like **agnolotti** (Piedmontese ravioli) filled with roasted meat and **hazelnut cake** for dessert.

Day 5: Piedmont to Emilia-Romagna – The Land of Parmesan and Balsamic Vinegar

- **Morning**: Travel to **Bologna**, the capital of **Emilia-Romagna**, a region famous for its culinary heritage. Start your day with a **food tour** of the **Quadrilatero Market**, where you'll sample local products like **Mortadella, Bologna's signature salami**, and freshly made **tortellini**.
    - **Address**: Via Clavature, 12, 40124 Bologna BO, Italy
- **Afternoon**: Visit a **Parmigiano Reggiano** dairy farm in the countryside. Watch how the cheese is made, and sample different ages of the famous **Parmesan**.
    - **Farm Tour: Caseificio di Montagna**
    - **Address**: Via Cà Paja, 40060 Bologna BO, Italy
    - **Ticket Price**: €15-€30 for a guided tour and tasting.
- **Evening**: Enjoy a traditional **Bolognese dinner** at **Trattoria di Via Serra**, where you can taste **tagliatelle al ragù** (the original Bolognese sauce) paired with a glass of local **Sangiovese** .

Day 6: Bologna to Modena – Balsamic Vinegar Heaven

- **Morning**: Visit **Modena**, the birthplace of **Balsamic Vinegar**. Take a guided tour of a **traditional balsamic vinegar producer**, where you will learn how this world-renowned condiment is crafted and aged in wooden barrels.
    - **Vinegar Producer: Acetaia Malpighi**
    - **Address**: Via Roncaglio, 21, 41051 Castelnuovo Rangone MO, Italy
    - **Ticket Price**: €25-€40 for a tasting tour.
- **Afternoon**: Explore Modena's historic center and visit **Osteria Francescana**, home to renowned chef **Massimo Bottura**, where you can indulge in Michelin-starred dishes.
    - **Address**: Via Stella, 22, 41121 Modena MO, Italy

- **Evening**: Dinner at **Osteria Stallo del Pomodoro**, known for its traditional **lasagne verdi** (green lasagna with spinach and ragù) and **torta di Modena** (Modena cake).

Day 7: Emilia-Romagna to Tuscany – Tuscan Culinary Delights

- **Morning**: Travel to **Florence**, Tuscany's capital. Start your Tuscan culinary adventure with a visit to the **Mercato Centrale** for a **food tour** that includes local specialties like **lampredotto** (a traditional Florentine sandwich), **pecorino cheese**, and **Chianti** .
- **Afternoon**: Take a Tuscan **cooking class** and learn how to prepare dishes like **pappardelle al cinghiale** (wild boar pasta) and **ribollita** (a hearty vegetable and bread soup).
- **Evening**: Dine at **Trattoria Sostanza**, a local favorite serving **pollo al burro** (butter chicken) and classic **Florentine steak**.

Day 8: Tuscany – and Olive Oil in Chianti

- **Morning**: Visit a **Chianti ry** for a -tasting tour, where you can sample some of the best **Chianti Classico** s paired with olive oils produced on the estate.
  - ry: **Castello di Verrazzano**
  - **Address**: Strada di Citille, 56, 50020 Greve in Chianti FI, Italy
  - **Ticket Price**: €25-€45 for a tour and tasting.
- **Afternoon**: Take a leisurely **vineyard walk** in the rolling hills of Chianti, learning about production and the importance of the Tuscan climate and soil.
- **Evening**: Return to Florence for a gourmet dinner at **Cibrèo**, a renowned Tuscan restaurant offering elevated regional dishes like **tuscan tripe stew** and **panforte** (a traditional spiced cake).

Day 9: Florence to Lake Garda – Italian Alps and Local Flavors

- **Morning**: Travel to **Lake Garda**, a picturesque area known for its mix of alpine and Mediterranean cuisine. Start your day with a visit to a **local olive oil mill** and taste the region's famous **Lago di Garda olive oil**.
- **Afternoon**: Explore **Sirmione**, a charming lakeside town, and enjoy a **lake fish-tasting lunch** featuring local delicacies such as **trota** (trout) and **coregone** (a freshwater fish).
- **Evening**: Visit a **local ry** around the lake and enjoy a -tasting session featuring **Lugana** and **Bardolino** s.

Day 10: Departure from Verona

- **Morning**: Spend your last morning in **Verona**, exploring its beautiful historical center and stopping by **Piazza delle Erbe** for some final gourmet shopping.
- **Afternoon**: Enjoy a **final meal** at **Ristorante Antica Torre**, where you can try classic dishes such as **bigoli in salsa** (long pasta with anchovy sauce) and **tiramisu**, the famous Italian dessert.
- **Evening**: Depart from Verona, taking with you the flavors of Northern Italy.

Additional Tips

- **Booking Tours**: Reserve cooking classes, tours, and culinary experiences in advance, especially during peak travel seasons (spring and autumn).
- **Local Markets**: Don't miss visiting local markets like the **Mercato Centrale** in Florence, **Piazza delle Erbe** in Verona, and **Mercato di Porta Palazzo** in Turin for fresh, regional produce.
- **Weather**: Northern Italy can be hot in summer, so pack light, breathable clothing and stay hydrated. The cooler spring and fall months are ideal for food-related travel.

This 10-day culinary adventure will immerse you in the flavors of Northern Italy, where each region offers its own culinary treasures, from truffles and to cheese and olive oil. Whether you're learning to cook traditional pasta, tasting world-class s, or enjoying local specialties, this journey is a food lover's dream.

9.3 A 14-Day Comprehensive Road Trip Through Northern Italy

Embark on a 14-day road trip through Northern Italy, where stunning landscapes, historical cities, and regional cuisine await at every turn. This journey covers iconic cities, quaint villages, picturesque lakes, and the majestic Alps, all while offering an immersive experience into Northern Italy's culture, cuisine, and heritage.

Day 1: Arrival in Milan – The Fashion Capital

- **Morning**: Arrive in **Milan**, Northern Italy's vibrant metropolis. Start your day with a visit to **Duomo di Milano**, Milan's grand cathedral, and climb to the rooftop for panoramic views of the city.
    - **Ticket Price**: €10-€15
    - **Website**: Duomo Milano
- **Afternoon**: Take a stroll through the **Galleria Vittorio Emanuele II**, Italy's oldest shopping mall, and enjoy a coffee at one of the historic cafes.

- **Evening**: Dinner at **Ristorante Cracco**, a Michelin-starred restaurant that offers contemporary Italian cuisine.

Day 2: Milan to Lake Como – Scenic Escape

- **Morning**: Pick up your rental car and drive to **Lake Como**, a scenic 1.5-hour drive. Stop at **Como** for a leisurely walk along the lakeside and a visit to the **Como Cathedral**.
- **Afternoon**: Take a boat tour of **Lake Como**, stopping at picturesque villages like **Bellagio** and **Varenna**. Enjoy lunch by the lake, savoring **risotto con pesce persico** (perch fish risotto), a regional specialty.
- **Evening**: Dinner at **Il Gatto Nero**, an upscale restaurant overlooking the lake, known for its Italian classics and fresh lake fish.

Day 3: Lake Como to Bergamo – Medieval Charm

- **Morning**: Head to **Bergamo** (1.5-hour drive), a charming medieval town. Explore **Città Alta** (Upper Town) and walk through its cobblestone streets, visiting **Piazza Vecchia** and **Basilica di Santa Maria Maggiore**.
  - **Ticket Price**: Free entry to the piazza; Basilica entry €3
- **Afternoon**: Visit **Accademia Carrara**, one of Italy's finest art museums, with a collection that includes works by Bellini, Titian, and Raphael.
  - **Ticket Price**: €10
  - **Website**: Accademia Carrara
- **Evening**: Dinner at **Da Mimmo**, a local restaurant known for its traditional **casoncelli** (stuffed pasta).

Day 4: Bergamo to Verona – Shakespeare's Romance

- **Morning**: Drive to **Verona** (1.5-hour drive). Upon arrival, visit **Casa di Giulietta**, Juliet's House, and the famous **balcony**.
  - **Ticket Price**: €6
- **Afternoon**: Explore **Piazza delle Erbe** and the **Verona Arena**, an ancient Roman amphitheater that still hosts operatic performances.
  - **Ticket Price**: €10
- **Evening**: Dinner at **Antica Bottega del Vino**, a traditional osteria offering local s and specialties like **risotto al tastasal** (pork sausage risotto).

Day 5: Verona to Venice – The City of Canals

- **Morning**: Drive to **Venice** (1.5-hour drive). Park your car at a designated parking area and take a vaporetto (water bus) to **Piazza San Marco**. Visit **St. Mark's Basilica** and climb the bell tower for spectacular views of the city.

- - Ticket Price: €6 for Basilica; €10 for Bell Tower
  - Website: St. Mark's Basilica
- **Afternoon**: Explore **Rialto Bridge** and stroll through the narrow streets and canals of **Cannaregio**.
- **Evening**: Dinner at **Osteria alle Testiere**, a popular seafood restaurant in Venice, offering **fritto misto** (mixed fried seafood).

Day 6: Venice to Padua – A Day in the Ancient City

- **Morning**: Drive to **Padua** (1-hour drive), home to one of the oldest universities in Europe. Visit the **Scrovegni Chapel**, renowned for its frescoes by Giotto.
  - Ticket Price: €13
  - Website: Scrovegni Chapel
- **Afternoon**: Explore **Prato della Valle**, one of Europe's largest squares, and the **Basilica di Sant'Antonio**, an impressive pilgrimage site.
- **Evening**: Dinner at **Ristorante Antico Mercato**, offering delicious Venetian-style fish and local s.

Day 7: Padua to Bologna – Culinary Capital of Italy

- **Morning**: Drive to **Bologna** (1-hour drive). Explore the historic city center, starting with **Piazza Maggiore** and the iconic **Two Towers**.
  - Ticket Price: €3 for the Torre degli Asinelli
- **Afternoon**: Visit **Mercato di Mezzo**, a bustling food market where you can sample **mortadella**, **tagliatelle al ragù**, and **tortellini**.
- **Evening**: Dinner at **Trattoria di Via Serra**, known for its classic Bolognese dishes and excellent local s.

Day 8: Bologna to Florence – The Heart of the Renaissance

- **Morning**: Drive to **Florence** (1-hour drive). Start by visiting the **Piazza del Duomo**, where you'll see the majestic **Cathedral of Santa Maria del Fiore**, **Giotto's Campanile**, and the **Baptistery of St. John**.
  - Ticket Price: €15 for the cathedral complex
- **Afternoon**: Visit the **Uffizi Gallery**, home to Renaissance masterpieces by Botticelli, Leonardo da Vinci, and Michelangelo.
  - Ticket Price: €20
  - Website: Uffizi Gallery
- **Evening**: Dinner at **Osteria All'Antico Vinaio**, famous for its Tuscan sandwiches and **ribollita**.

Day 9: Florence to Pisa – The Leaning Tower

- **Morning**: Drive to **Pisa** (1-hour drive). Visit the iconic **Leaning Tower of Pisa** and the **Piazza dei Miracoli**, home to the cathedral and baptistery.
    - **Ticket Price**: €20 for tower and cathedral
- **Afternoon**: Stroll along **Corso Italia** and sample the local **cecina** (chickpea pancake).
- **Evening**: Return to **Florence** for a gourmet dinner at **Cibrèo**, offering a modern twist on Tuscan classics.

Day 10: Florence to Lucca – A Day of Charming Villages

- **Morning**: Drive to **Lucca** (1-hour drive). Explore the well-preserved medieval town center, visiting the **Piazza dell'Anfiteatro** and **Lucca Cathedral**.
- **Afternoon**: Walk or bike around the **city walls**, which date back to the 16th century.
- **Evening**: Dinner at **Trattoria Da Leo**, where you can try local specialties like **tordelli lucchesi** (stuffed pasta).

Day 11: Lucca to Cinque Terre – Coastal Beauty

- **Morning**: Drive to **Cinque Terre** (2.5-hour drive). Start with the village of **Monterosso al Mare** and enjoy the beautiful coastal views.
- **Afternoon**: Take a boat or hiking tour connecting the five villages of **Cinque Terre**.
- **Evening**: Dinner at **Ristorante Miky**, offering Ligurian specialties like **trofie al pesto** (pasta with pesto sauce).

Day 12: Cinque Terre to Genoa – Maritime History

- **Morning**: Drive to **Genoa** (1.5-hour drive). Explore the **Palazzo Ducale** and stroll through the **Porto Antico** (Old Harbor).
- **Afternoon**: Visit the **Genoa Aquarium**, one of Europe's largest aquariums.
    - **Ticket Price**: €15
- **Evening**: Dinner at **Ristorante Zeffirino**, known for its fresh seafood and Ligurian cuisine.

Day 13: Genoa to Milan – Return to the Fashion Capital

- **Morning**: Drive back to **Milan** (2-hour drive). Spend your final day exploring **Brera District**, home to art galleries, boutiques, and cafes.
- **Afternoon**: Visit **Pinacoteca di Brera**, a gallery housing works by Caravaggio and Raphael.

- ○ **Ticket Price**: €15
- **Evening**: Dinner at **Nobu Milano**, a fusion of Japanese and Italian culinary influences.

Day 14: Departure from Milan

- **Morning**: After breakfast, head to **Milano Centrale** for your departure.

Final Thoughts

This 14-day comprehensive road trip through Northern Italy allows you to explore a perfect blend of historical cities, coastal beauty, cultural landmarks, and of course, incredible food and . Whether you're a history buff, nature enthusiast, or foodie, this itinerary has something for everyone. Make sure to savor the regional specialties at every stop, from **Tuscany's and olive oil** to **Piedmont's truffles** and **Venetian seafood**. Safe travels and buon appetito!

Chapter 10. Practical Information

10.1 Currency Exchange and Banking

When traveling to Northern Italy in 2025, it is important to understand the local currency exchange and banking systems to ensure a smooth financial experience throughout your trip. Here's a detailed guide to help you navigate currency exchange and banking in Italy.

Currency Used in Northern Italy

- **Official Currency**: The official currency of Italy is the **Euro (€)**.
- **Coins**: Euro coins are used in denominations of €1, €2, 1 cent, 2 cents, 5 cents, 10 cents, 20 cents, and 50 cents.
- **Banknotes**: Banknotes come in denominations of €5, €10, €20, €50, €100, €200, and €500.

Currency Exchange

- **Currency Exchange Offices**: In major cities like Milan, Venice, and Florence, currency exchange offices (often called "Cambio") are readily available. These can be found in popular tourist areas, airports, and train stations. However, exchange rates at these locations might not be the most favorable, and there could be commission fees involved.

  - **Tip**: Avoid exchanging currency at airports if possible, as rates are usually worse.

- **Currency Exchange at Banks**: Banks also offer currency exchange services, although some may only exchange foreign currency if you hold an account with them. It is advisable to visit a bank with an international presence for better rates.

- **ATMs**: **ATMs** are widely available throughout Italy, especially in cities and towns. They typically offer the most competitive exchange rates, though you may be subject to foreign transaction fees depending on your bank's policies. It's always advisable to notify your bank about your travel dates to prevent your card from being blocked due to suspicious activity.

  - **Tip**: Use ATMs that are located near major banks for a secure exchange and to avoid additional charges. Opt for **Visa** or **Mastercard** affiliated ATMs for ease of use.

Credit and Debit Cards

- **Widely Accepted**: Major credit and debit cards (such as **Visa**, **Mastercard**, and **American Express**) are widely accepted in Italy, particularly in larger cities, tourist areas, and at most hotels, restaurants, and stores.
- **Card Payments**: Card payments are common, and many places prefer or even require cards for larger transactions. However, always have a small amount of cash for places that may not accept cards, such as small cafes, shops, or rural areas.
- **Chip and PIN**: Italy uses the **chip and PIN** method for card payments, so ensure your cards are equipped with this feature. Be prepared to use your PIN when making payments.
- **Foreign Transaction Fees**: Some banks charge a fee for international card transactions. It's a good idea to check with your bank before your trip about these fees and whether they offer fee-free international transactions.

Opening Hours for Banks and ATMs

- **Bank Hours**: Banks in Italy typically open from **8:30 AM to 1:30 PM** on weekdays and **3:00 PM to 4:00 PM** in the afternoon. They close on **Saturdays** and **Sundays**.
    - **Tip**: Be sure to plan ahead if you need to exchange currency or withdraw large amounts, as many banks are closed on weekends.
- **ATM Availability**: ATMs are available 24/7 in most cities, and you can withdraw money at any time. However, note that some ATMs may limit the withdrawal amount per transaction, especially in smaller towns.

Banking in Italy

- **Opening an Account**: If you plan to stay in Italy for an extended period, you may want to open a local bank account. This process typically requires proof of identity (passport), proof of residence, and sometimes proof of income or employment.
- **Common Banks**: Some of the main banking institutions in Italy include:
    - **UniCredit**: A large bank with branches in major cities.
    - **Intesa Sanpaolo**: One of Italy's largest banks with a wide network of branches.
    - **Banco di Sardegna**: A bank with more regional offerings, primarily in Sardinia.
    - **UBI Banca**: Provides services throughout Northern Italy.

Tipping and Service Charges

- **Tipping in Restaurants**: While tipping is not obligatory in Italy, it is appreciated for good service. In restaurants, a **service charge** may already be included in your bill. If it's not, a tip of **5-10%** is customary for good service. However, it's not necessary to tip large amounts in Italy.
- **Tipping Taxi Drivers**: Taxi drivers in Italy do not expect tips, but rounding up the fare is common practice for small change.
- **Tipping in Hotels**: Hotel staff, such as bellhops, may be tipped **€1-€2** per bag, and housekeeping staff can be tipped **€1-€2** per night if you are staying in higher-end hotels.

Foreign Exchange Fees and Charges

- **Foreign Transaction Fees**: Before using your cards abroad, check whether your bank imposes a **foreign transaction fee**. Some credit cards, especially those with a focus on international travelers, offer **no foreign transaction fees**.
- **Exchange Rate Fluctuations**: Exchange rates can fluctuate due to various factors, so it's worth monitoring them before and during your trip. Several smartphone apps, such as **XE Currency** or **Revolut**, can help you keep track of the latest rates.

When traveling in Northern Italy, there are plenty of options for handling money and making payments. ATMs offer the best exchange rates, but it's essential to be mindful of your bank's fees. Credit and debit cards are widely accepted, though always carry some cash for smaller purchases, especially in rural areas. Understanding Italy's banking hours and customs around tipping can help ensure your financial experience is as smooth as possible.

10.2 Emergency Services and Health Care

When traveling in Northern Italy in 2025, it is essential to be aware of emergency services and healthcare options. Understanding how to access medical care and emergency services can provide peace of mind during your trip. This section will guide you through the key healthcare facilities, emergency numbers, and advice on staying safe and healthy while traveling.

Emergency Services in Northern Italy

In the case of an emergency, Northern Italy has a robust and efficient system in place to assist both locals and tourists. Here's a breakdown of essential emergency services:

Emergency Numbers

- **General Emergency (Police, Ambulance, Fire)**: **112** (EU-wide emergency number)

    o This is the standard emergency number in Italy, and it will connect you to police, fire, and medical services.
    o **Note**: Call this number for any urgent emergency, such as accidents, medical conditions, fires, or crimes in progress.

- **Ambulance**: **118**

    o If you need an ambulance or medical assistance, dial **118** directly to request immediate medical attention.

- **Police**: **113**

    o For any situation involving crime, accidents, or safety concerns, call the police directly at **113**.

- **Fire Department**: **115**

    o If there's a fire or you need fire-fighting services, you can reach the fire department by calling **115**.

- **Medical Emergency Services**:

    o If you need urgent medical advice but are unsure whether it's a true emergency, some regions in Italy offer medical services that can be called directly. In many cities, **pronto soccorso** (emergency medical service) departments at hospitals are available for non-life-threatening issues.

Healthcare and Medical Assistance

Italy boasts a high standard of healthcare, and there are various options for tourists in need of medical care. Here's what you need to know about health services in Northern Italy:

Public Healthcare System

- **Public Health Insurance**: Italy's public healthcare system, known as **Servizio Sanitario Nazionale (SSN)**, provides universal healthcare for residents. Tourists visiting Italy on a short-term basis will typically need private health insurance or may be able to access emergency care under EU agreements.

- **EU Citizens**: If you are an EU citizen, bring your **European Health Insurance Card (EHIC)**. This allows you to access state-provided healthcare during your stay, typically at a reduced cost or for free, depending on the situation.

- **Non-EU Citizens**: Travelers from non-EU countries are advised to have **travel insurance** that includes medical coverage. Some hospitals may ask for payment upfront for non-emergency care if you do not have travel insurance or a valid European Health Insurance Card.

- **Public Hospitals**: Public hospitals are available throughout Northern Italy, with well-trained staff and modern medical facilities. While emergency care is free for EU residents with the EHIC, non-residents may be asked to pay for services upfront, particularly for non-urgent care.

    - **Major Hospitals in Northern Italy**:
        - **Ospedale Niguarda** (Milan)
        - **Ospedale di Cisanello** (Pisa)
        - **Ospedale Maggiore** (Bologna)
        - **Ospedale San Giovanni** (Verona)

- **Pharmacies**: Pharmacies (**farmacia**) are widely available in cities and towns across Northern Italy. You can find them on almost every street corner in urban areas. Most pharmacies will carry over-the-counter medications and can also provide medical advice for minor health issues, such as colds or injuries.

    - **Green Cross Sign**: Look for the green cross sign, which marks a pharmacy.
    - **Pharmacy Hours**: Pharmacies in larger cities are usually open Monday to Saturday, from **8:30 AM to 1:00 PM** and then from **4:00 PM to 7:30 PM**. In small towns, some pharmacies may close for a longer lunch break. On Sundays, pharmacies may have rotating hours or be closed.

Private Healthcare and Clinics

For faster or more specialized treatment, private clinics and healthcare facilities are available in Northern Italy. These facilities may be more expensive than public healthcare, but they often offer quicker access to medical professionals and private rooms.

- **Private Hospitals**: Some well-known private hospitals include **Clinica Città Studi** in Milan and **Policlinico San Donato** in Milan.

- **General Practitioners (GPs)**: If you require non-emergency medical care, you can make an appointment with a private general practitioner or family doctor. Private clinics and GPs may accept walk-ins or appointments, but it's always best to schedule in advance.

Medications and Prescriptions

- **Prescriptions**: If you require prescription medications, you can fill your prescription at any pharmacy. Some medications that are available over-the-counter in your home country may require a prescription in Italy.
    - **Foreign Prescriptions**: If you have a prescription from your home country, most pharmacies can fulfill the prescription if it's in English or Italian. However, some may need you to obtain an Italian prescription.
- **Over-the-Counter Medications**: Pharmacies in Italy carry a wide variety of over-the-counter medications for common ailments such as headaches, colds, allergies, and digestive issues.

Health and Safety Tips

- **Travel Insurance**: It is highly recommended that all travelers have comprehensive travel insurance that covers medical expenses, accidents, and repatriation. This will provide additional peace of mind in case you need medical care during your visit.
- **Vaccinations**: There are no mandatory vaccinations for entry into Italy, but it is advisable to be up to date with routine vaccinations (like tetanus, measles, and influenza) before traveling.
- **Water Safety**: Tap water in Italy is generally safe to drink. However, if you're in rural areas, bottled water may be recommended. Many restaurants will offer bottled water upon request, but it's typically charged.
- **Health Emergency Cards**: Carry a card with the details of your insurance, emergency contacts, and any specific medical conditions or allergies you may have. This will assist medical professionals in the event of an emergency.

Northern Italy offers reliable and high-quality healthcare options for travelers. Familiarizing yourself with emergency services, knowing the emergency numbers, and ensuring you have proper travel insurance can make dealing with medical situations smoother and less stressful. Whether you need minor medical assistance, emergency care, or more specialized treatment, Italy's healthcare system is designed to provide timely and professional services. Always be prepared, especially when it comes to ensuring you have adequate health coverage during your travels.

10.3 Safety Tips for Travelers

Northern Italy is a beautiful and relatively safe destination for travelers, offering a blend of culture, natural beauty, and rich history. However, like any travel destination, it's important to be aware of certain safety measures to ensure a smooth and enjoyable trip. Here's a comprehensive guide on how to stay safe while exploring Northern Italy.

General Safety Tips

1. **Stay Aware of Your Surroundings**:

   - **Be mindful of your belongings**, especially in crowded tourist spots such as Milan's Duomo, Venice's St. Mark's Square, and Florence's Uffizi Gallery. Pickpockets are known to target tourists in busy areas or on public transport.
   - Avoid distractions like looking at your phone or carrying large amounts of cash in public.

2. **Stay in Well-Lit Areas**:

   - Stick to well-lit and populated areas, especially at night. Avoid walking in isolated areas after dark, particularly in major cities.
   - In smaller towns and rural areas, it's a good idea to familiarize yourself with your surroundings before venturing out after dark.

3. **Use Reliable Transportation**:

   - Use reputable taxi services or ride-sharing apps like **Uber** in cities. Always make sure the vehicle is registered before entering.
   - If you're using public transportation, keep an eye on your belongings at train stations, bus stops, and on board.

4. **Avoid Scams**:

   - Watch out for street vendors selling counterfeit goods or offering "free" items like friendship bracelets. If you don't want them, politely decline and move on.
   - Be cautious of people approaching you on the streets, offering unsolicited help or directions, as some may be trying to scam you.

5. **Emergency Contacts**:

   - Keep a list of emergency contact numbers in case of an urgent situation. This includes local police, your embassy, and a nearby hospital.

- It's a good idea to have a printed copy of these numbers in addition to digital copies on your phone.

Health and Medical Safety

1. **Travel Insurance**:

    - Before traveling, ensure that you have **comprehensive travel insurance** that covers medical emergencies, accidents, and theft. Always have your insurance details easily accessible.

2. **Medication and Allergies**:

    - If you take prescription medication, carry enough for the duration of your trip. Ensure that you have a copy of the prescription in case you need to replace your medication while traveling.
    - If you have allergies (especially food allergies), make sure to communicate this clearly when dining out or purchasing food.

3. **Sun Protection**:

    - Northern Italy can experience hot summers, especially in cities like Milan, Verona, and Florence. Always wear **sunscreen**, sunglasses, and a hat, and stay hydrated to avoid heat-related illnesses.

4. **Drinking Water**:

    - Tap water in Italy is generally safe to drink. However, if you're in more rural areas or unsure of the water quality, stick to bottled water.

Personal Security Tips

1. **Money and Cards**:

    - Carry a **credit card** or **debit card** for most transactions and avoid carrying large amounts of cash.
    - Use a **money belt** or **anti-theft bag** to store valuables securely. Many pickpockets operate in crowded tourist areas, so always keep your bag close to your body and zipped up.
    - If you lose your wallet or cards, immediately report it to your bank and cancel your credit cards.

2. **Safe Accommodation Choices**:

    o Choose accommodation that has good reviews and is in a reputable location. Check online platforms like **Booking.com** or **Airbnb** for guest feedback.
    o For added security, opt for hotels with 24-hour reception and secure locks or safes for valuables.

3. **Taxi and Ride-Sharing Safety**:

    o Only use official taxi ranks or well-known ride-sharing apps. Avoid accepting rides from people approaching you on the street, especially late at night.
    o Always verify the identity of the driver and the vehicle before entering.

Safety in the Cities

1. **Milan**:

    o While Milan is a cosmopolitan city with a relatively low crime rate, areas around the **Central Station** and **Brera District** may see higher levels of petty crime. Remain vigilant when walking through these areas, especially at night.
    o Always use **reputable taxis** or public transportation rather than accepting rides from unmarked cars.

2. **Venice**:

    o Venice can be crowded, especially in the summer, making it a hotspot for pickpockets. Keep an eye on your belongings, particularly in areas like **Rialto Bridge** and **St. Mark's Square**.
    o Avoid walking in empty alleys late at night, especially near the less touristy areas of the city.

3. **Florence**:

    o The historic center of Florence is generally safe, but be cautious of pickpockets in crowded places like the **Piazza del Duomo** or **Ponte Vecchio**.
    o If you're planning to explore Florence's less crowded areas, ensure you're familiar with the layout of the city beforehand.

4. **Verona**:

    - Verona is known for being relatively safe, but like any popular tourist destination, keep your belongings secure in crowded areas such as **Piazza delle Erbe** and the **Arena di Verona**.
    - Avoid any street performers or beggars who might be working in groups and distracting you.

Safety in the Countryside and Natural Areas

1. **The Italian Alps**:

    - If you plan to visit the **Dolomites** or the **Italian Alps**, ensure you are adequately prepared for outdoor activities. Check weather forecasts regularly, and carry a map and compass when hiking or skiing.
    - Always stay on marked trails and, if unsure about routes, consider hiring a local guide.
    - **Mountain Rescue**: In case of an emergency, call **118** or use the local mountain rescue service, which operates 24/7.

2. **Lakes Region**:

    - The lakes in Northern Italy, including **Lake Como** and **Lake Garda**, are beautiful for boating and water activities. Always follow safety guidelines provided by rental companies for any water-based excursions.
    - Ensure your boat is equipped with life jackets and that you are familiar with local regulations regarding water activities.

Traveling by Car

1. **Driving in Italy**:
    - If you're renting a car in Northern Italy, always follow **traffic laws** and be aware that in cities like Milan and Venice, **ZTL (Limited Traffic Zones)** restrict car access to certain areas. Ensure you understand these zones to avoid fines.
    - **Parking**: Parking can be challenging in larger cities, so always park in designated areas and be wary of any scam parking attendants. Use official parking lots or garages where possible.
    - **Speed Limits**: Italy has strict speed limits. In urban areas, it's generally **50 km/h**, and on highways, it's **130 km/h**. Always adhere to the posted signs.

While Northern Italy is a safe destination for travelers, it's important to stay vigilant and take basic precautions to ensure your safety. By being aware of your surroundings, following common-sense safety measures, and planning ahead, you can enjoy a secure and memorable trip to this beautiful region. Always carry important documents, emergency contacts, and health information with you, and don't hesitate to seek help if needed.

Chapter 11. Sustainable Travel

11.1 Eco-Friendly Travel Tips

As the world becomes increasingly aware of the environmental impact of travel, more tourists are choosing sustainable ways to explore the globe. Northern Italy, with its breathtaking landscapes, rich culture, and commitment to conservation, offers plenty of opportunities for eco-conscious travelers to reduce their environmental footprint. Below are some detailed tips to help you travel sustainably while enjoying all the beauty that Northern Italy has to offer.

1. Choose Sustainable Accommodation

1. **Look for Eco-Friendly Hotels**:

   - Many hotels in Northern Italy are adopting **green certifications**, such as the **Green Key** or **EcoLabel**. These certifications indicate that the hotel follows practices aimed at reducing environmental impact. Look for accommodations that use energy-efficient lighting, water-saving measures, and sustainable materials in their construction and furnishings.
   - **Eco-Lodges and Agriturismos**: Stay in **agritourism** accommodations (agriturismos) or rural lodges. These places often focus on sustainable farming practices, offer local and organic food, and promote a connection with nature.

2. **Opt for Smaller, Independent Lodgings**:

   - Smaller, locally owned hotels or guesthouses are often more environmentally conscious than large chain hotels. Many focus on reducing waste, conserving energy, and supporting the local community.
   - **Family-run guesthouses** and **bed-and-breakfasts** often use local produce, reducing the carbon footprint associated with food transportation.

2. Use Public Transportation and Green Mobility

1. **Public Transport**:

   - Northern Italy has an excellent network of **trains**, **buses**, and **metros** that can reduce your carbon footprint compared to renting a car. Trains are a particularly eco-friendly way to travel long distances, with

high-speed options such as the **Frecciarossa** and **Italo** trains offering efficient, fast, and relatively low-emission transportation.
- Many cities, such as Milan and Venice, also have extensive **public transport** systems that allow you to get around without the need for a car. Trams, buses, and metros are readily available and relatively affordable.

2. **Renting a Bicycle**:

- In cities like Milan, Florence, and Venice, **bike rentals** are available, and the cities are becoming more bike-friendly with designated bike lanes. Using a bike is an excellent way to reduce your carbon footprint while exploring urban areas at your own pace.
- Consider taking a **guided bike tour** to explore the local history and culture while minimizing your environmental impact.

3. **Electric Scooters and Cars**:

- Many Italian cities have adopted the use of **electric scooters** for short-distance travel. These scooters are available through apps such as **Lime** and **Circ**, which help reduce emissions compared to traditional gasoline-powered vehicles.
- For those looking to rent a car, choose an **electric or hybrid vehicle** if possible. Major car rental agencies in Northern Italy, including in Milan and Venice, offer eco-friendly options.

3. Be Mindful of Your Consumption

1. **Reduce Single-Use Plastics**:

- **Avoid single-use plastic bottles** by bringing your own reusable water bottle. In many cities, you'll find public water fountains with clean drinking water, allowing you to refill your bottle.
- Carry a **reusable shopping bag** to reduce the need for plastic bags when purchasing goods or food. Northern Italy, like much of Europe, is increasingly moving toward a reduction in plastic use, but it's always a good idea to be proactive.

2. **Support Local, Sustainable Products**:

- Northern Italy is renowned for its local and organic food, from the **Trentino-Alto Adige region's apples** to **Emilia-Romagna's organic Parmigiano Reggiano**. When dining, look for restaurants or markets that source ingredients locally and sustainably.

- Purchase artisanal goods, such as locally made leather products, , or cheeses, from smaller producers who engage in ethical practices and support the local economy.
3. **Eat Seasonally**:

    - Northern Italy has a rich culinary tradition that embraces seasonal produce. Eating seasonal food is more environmentally friendly as it reduces the need for imported goods and lessens the carbon footprint of transportation.
    - **Farm-to-table restaurants** are a great option to support sustainable food systems. Many places will also offer vegetarian and vegan options, which generally have a lower environmental impact than meat-heavy meals.

4. **Minimize Waste and Recycle**

    1. **Be Conscious of Waste**:

        - Italians are serious about recycling, and Northern Italy is no exception. Many cities have dedicated bins for **separate waste disposal**—including paper, plastic, glass, and organic waste—so make sure to sort your trash accordingly.
        - **Refuse unnecessary packaging** when shopping or eating out. For example, bring your own container to avoid takeaway packaging when buying food or souvenirs.

    2. **Take Part in Sustainability Programs**:

        - Many accommodations, tourist attractions, and restaurants are involved in sustainability programs. Look for those that use **energy-efficient lighting**, **solar power**, or **eco-friendly cleaning products**. Participating in these programs can help reduce your environmental footprint.

    3. **Respect Local Natural Resources**:

        - Avoid littering or disturbing natural spaces, especially when visiting outdoor destinations such as the **Italian Alps** or **Lake Garda**. Follow all **leave-no-trace principles** to help preserve Italy's stunning natural beauty for future generations.

5. Support Sustainable Tourism Initiatives

1. **Responsible Wildlife and Nature Tourism**:

   - Northern Italy offers incredible nature experiences, from hiking in the **Dolomites** to exploring the shores of **Lake Como**. To ensure these environments remain preserved, support **eco-tourism operators** who prioritize conservation efforts and sustainability.
   - Participate in **wildlife conservation programs** or visit **national parks** that focus on the protection of local flora and fauna.

2. **Ethical Tour Operators**:

   - When booking guided tours or experiences, choose companies that focus on **sustainable practices**, including responsible wildlife viewing, minimal environmental impact, and support for local communities.
   - Some companies in Northern Italy offer **eco-friendly tours** that focus on history, culture, or food while reducing environmental impact.

3. **Carbon Offsetting**:

   - If your travel to Northern Italy involves long flights, consider **carbon offset programs** offered by airlines or independent organizations. These programs invest in environmental projects that help reduce the carbon footprint of your trip, such as reforestation or renewable energy initiatives.

6. Visit Sustainable Attractions

1. **Eco-Friendly Museums and Attractions**:

   - Many museums and attractions in Northern Italy are dedicated to sustainability and environmental education. For example, the **Museo della Scienza e della Tecnologia** in Milan promotes environmental awareness through exhibits on sustainable technologies.
   - Look for eco-certified cultural sites and attractions, which aim to reduce energy consumption, waste, and water usage.

2. **Green Spaces and Parks**:

   - Northern Italy is home to beautiful parks and gardens that focus on conservation and sustainable maintenance. Explore **Parco Sempione** in Milan or the **Botanical Garden of Brera** in Venice, both of which highlight sustainable landscaping practices.

By incorporating these eco-friendly travel tips into your Northern Italy adventure, you'll not only reduce your environmental footprint but also contribute to the preservation of the region's unique cultural and natural heritage. From using public transport and supporting local businesses to staying in sustainable accommodations and respecting local ecosystems, every small choice you make helps promote a greener and more sustainable way of traveling. Northern Italy offers travelers a chance to explore its beauty while leaving a positive impact on the environment and its communities.

11.2 Supporting Local Communities

Traveling responsibly in Northern Italy means not only caring for the environment but also supporting the communities you visit. By making conscious choices, you can contribute to the well-being of the local people, preserve their cultural heritage, and help sustain the region's economy. This section will guide you on how to support local communities during your visit.

1. Choose Locally-Owned Accommodation

1. **Stay in Family-Owned Hotels and Guesthouses**:

    - Opt for locally-owned **bed-and-breakfasts** or **guesthouses** instead of large hotel chains. These smaller accommodations are often more involved in their communities and ensure that the majority of the revenue stays within the local economy.
    - Many family-run establishments also offer an authentic experience, providing travelers with personal insights into local culture and traditions.

2. **Agriturismos**:

    - Northern Italy is renowned for its agriturismo accommodations, which are family-run farms that combine hospitality with farming. Staying at these locations not only supports local farming families but also gives you a chance to experience Italy's agricultural heritage firsthand.
    - Many agriturismos serve farm-to-table meals and offer sustainable, locally sourced food, which helps maintain traditional farming practices while promoting rural development.

2. Support Local Artisans and Shops

1. **Buy Handmade Souvenirs**:

    - Rather than purchasing mass-produced souvenirs, consider supporting local artisans by buying handmade items. Northern Italy is famous for its

artisan goods, such as leather products from **Florence**, intricate glasswork from **Murano** (Venice), or handmade textiles from **Como**.
   - These unique, high-quality products are not only beautiful but also contribute to preserving traditional craftsmanship and skills that have been passed down through generations.
2. **Visit Local Markets**:
   - Explore **local markets** where you can purchase fresh produce, handmade goods, and artisanal food products directly from farmers and makers. Markets in cities like Milan, Venice, and Florence showcase local specialties, including cheeses, s, cured meats, and fresh produce. Shopping at these markets supports small-scale producers and ensures that your purchase has a direct positive impact on the local economy.
3. **Support Fair Trade Stores**:
   - If you're looking for products made ethically and sustainably, many cities in Northern Italy have **fair trade stores** where local and international artisans sell their goods. By purchasing from these shops, you're supporting fair wages and ethical working conditions.

3. Support Local Restaurants and Food Producers

1. **Eat at Family-Owned Restaurants**:
   - Choose **local restaurants**, **trattorias**, and **osterias** that are independently owned and operated. These establishments often focus on regional dishes and ingredients, supporting local farmers and food producers. By dining at these places, you're investing directly into the local food economy.
   - Ask about the restaurant's commitment to using **seasonal and local ingredients**. Many smaller restaurants in Northern Italy pride themselves on working with local farms, ensuring freshness while minimizing their carbon footprint.
2. **Participate in Culinary Experiences**:
   - Northern Italy is famous for its food and , and many regions offer **culinary experiences** that directly support local communities. For example, take a **cooking class** with a local chef, where you can learn to prepare traditional dishes using local ingredients. This supports the chef, local farmers, and the community while offering you an unforgettable cultural experience.

- Participate in **tastings** or visit **local vineyards** to learn about making techniques, purchase local , and meet the makers. Northern Italy is home to some of the finest regions, such as **Piedmont** and **Tuscany**, and visiting local vineyards helps support sustainable practices and small-scale production.

4. Hire Local Guides and Operators

1. **Choose Local Tour Operators**:

   - When planning tours or activities, select **local guides** and **tour operators** who have a deep knowledge of the region's history, culture, and geography. Local guides often offer personalized experiences and share insights that you might not find in guidebooks.
   - Hiring local guides for outdoor activities like hiking in the **Dolomites**, biking around **Lake Garda**, or taking walking tours in **Venice** ensures that the money spent stays within the community and supports those who make their living from tourism.

2. **Take Part in Sustainable and Community-Based Tours**:

   - Many tour operators in Northern Italy focus on **sustainable tourism** and work with local communities to create experiences that respect the environment and the culture. These tours often include visits to local farms, workshops, or sustainable projects that directly benefit the communities involved.

5. Contribute to Community Projects and Conservation Efforts

1. **Support Local Charities and NGOs**:

   - If you're passionate about giving back, consider donating to local charities or participating in community-based projects. Many local non-governmental organizations (NGOs) in Northern Italy focus on preserving local heritage, supporting disadvantaged communities, and promoting environmental conservation.
   - For example, organizations like **WWF Italy** focus on preserving Italy's natural landscapes, including the **Italian Alps** and **Mediterranean ecosystems**. Your donations can contribute to vital conservation efforts and help protect the region's biodiversity.

2. **Volunteer for Local Environmental Projects:**

    o For travelers with more time, consider volunteering with organizations that focus on **eco-tourism** and **cultural preservation**. Some local projects allow travelers to contribute their time and skills to restore cultural sites, clean up natural areas, or promote sustainable tourism practices in rural areas.

6. Promote Respect for Local Culture and Traditions

1. **Respect Local Customs and Traditions:**

    o Northern Italy is home to diverse cultures, from the alpine traditions of **Trentino-Alto Adige** to the Venetian culture of the **Veneto** region. Respecting local customs, dress codes, and traditions is crucial in promoting positive intercultural exchange.
    o For example, when visiting religious sites such as churches or cathedrals, dress modestly and follow local etiquette. In Venice, respect local initiatives to protect the **Venetian lagoon** by avoiding the use of motorized boats or contributing to the preservation of the fragile ecosystem.

2. **Avoid Over-Tourism:**

    o Avoid overcrowded tourist hotspots, especially during peak seasons, as this can strain local resources and negatively impact communities. Explore lesser-known areas to help distribute tourism income more evenly across the region. Towns like **Cortina d'Ampezzo**, **Bergamo**, and **Asolo** are beautiful and rich in history, but often less crowded than major cities like Milan or Venice.

7. Engage in Local Community Events and Festivals

1. **Attend Local Festivals:**

    o Participating in **local festivals** is a great way to support local communities while immersing yourself in their culture. Northern Italy hosts many annual festivals, such as the **Venice Carnival, Milan Fashion Week**, and **Verona Opera Festival**.
    o By attending these events, you not only support the local economy but also get a deeper understanding of the region's traditions, history, and people.

2. **Support Art and Culture**:

    - Many local art galleries, museums, and theaters are run by nonprofit organizations or local groups. Attending performances, exhibitions, or cultural events helps preserve traditional art forms and supports local artists.
    - In cities like Florence and Venice, you can visit **local artisan workshops**, where you can witness crafts like glass-blowing and leatherworking, and directly support the artisans.

By making thoughtful choices during your trip to Northern Italy, you can significantly contribute to the well-being of local communities. Whether you're choosing eco-friendly accommodations, supporting local businesses, or participating in community-based tourism, every action can have a positive impact. Northern Italy offers countless opportunities for travelers to engage with and support local cultures, fostering a deeper connection to the region and helping ensure that its traditions and resources are preserved for future generations.

Chapter 12. Day Trips and Hidden Gems

12.1 Off-the-Beaten-Path Destinations

Northern Italy is home to world-famous cities and attractions, but it also boasts hidden gems and lesser-known destinations that offer a more intimate and unique travel experience. If you're looking to escape the crowds and explore authentic locales, this section will guide you to some of the most intriguing off-the-beaten-path destinations in the region.

1. Cividale del Friuli – A Medieval Treasure

- **Location**: Friuli Venezia Giulia region, close to the Slovenian border
- **Why Visit**: Cividale del Friuli is a UNESCO World Heritage site that beautifully blends medieval history with stunning natural landscapes. The town is renowned for its **well-preserved medieval architecture**, including the **Ponte del Diavolo** (Devil's Bridge) and the **Tempietto Longobardo**, a Lombard-era chapel.
- **Highlights**:
    - The **Longobard Temple**: This UNESCO-listed chapel is a stunning example of Lombard architecture, built in the 8th century.
    - The **Ponte del Diavolo**: A medieval stone bridge that offers a picturesque spot for photos over the Natisone River.
    - The **National Archaeological Museum**: Features a collection of artifacts from the ancient Roman and Lombard periods.
- **Visitor Services**:
    - Guided tours are available through the town to learn about its rich medieval history.
    - Local cafes and restaurants serve traditional Friulian cuisine.

2. The Val Grande National Park – Untouched Wilderness

- **Location**: Piedmont region, near Lake Maggiore
- **Why Visit**: The **Val Grande National Park** is one of Italy's most remote and rugged wilderness areas, offering a tranquil escape for nature lovers and hikers. It's a perfect spot for those seeking solitude in the mountains and untouched landscapes.
- **Highlights**:
    - **Hiking Trails**: There are several challenging trails that take you deep into the park, offering breathtaking views of the surrounding mountains and valleys.

- - **Wildlife**: The park is home to a variety of wildlife, including deer, wild boar, and numerous bird species.
  - **Historical Sites**: Explore the ruins of abandoned villages like **Borgo di San Bernardino**, adding a historical touch to your adventure.
- **Visitor Services**:
  - **Hiking tours** with experienced guides are available to help visitors explore the park safely.
  - Visitor centers provide information about local flora, fauna, and conservation efforts.

3. Orta San Giulio – A Picturesque Lakeside Village

- **Location**: Piedmont region, Lake Orta
- **Why Visit**: Often overshadowed by the more famous Lake Como and Lake Maggiore, **Lake Orta** and its village, **Orta San Giulio**, is one of the most charming and peaceful lakeside spots in Northern Italy. The village's cobbled streets and serene atmosphere offer a glimpse of traditional Italian life.
- **Highlights**:
  - **Isola San Giulio**: A small, mystical island located just off the shore of Orta San Giulio, home to a Benedictine monastery. The island is accessible by boat and offers beautiful walking paths.
  - **Piazza Motta**: The village's main square, surrounded by colorful buildings and offering stunning views of Lake Orta.
  - **Sacro Monte di Orta**: A UNESCO World Heritage site with chapels that depict scenes from the life of St. Francis of Assisi.
- **Visitor Services**:
  - Boat rides to **Isola San Giulio** are popular, and guided tours are available.
  - Several **artisanal shops** and **cafes** in the village provide a local experience of Italian culture.

4. Bassano del Grappa – A Town of History and Grappa

- **Location**: Veneto region, near Vicenza
- **Why Visit**: Known for its famous **Grappa** (an Italian pomace brandy), **Bassano del Grappa** offers both a rich cultural history and stunning views of the surrounding mountains. The town is also renowned for its **wooden bridge**, **Ponte degli Alpini**, a symbol of the area.
- **Highlights**:
  - **Ponte degli Alpini**: A picturesque wooden bridge that crosses the Brenta River and is an iconic symbol of Bassano del Grappa.

- **Museo della Grappa**: A museum dedicated to the history and production of grappa, where visitors can learn about the distillation process and taste the local spirit.
    - **Historic Center**: Explore the medieval **Piazza Garibaldi** and the **Castello degli Ezzelini**, which offers panoramic views of the town.
- **Visitor Services**:
    - **Grappa distillery tours** are available in the surrounding area, where visitors can see the production process firsthand.
    - **Local restaurants** offer traditional dishes and, of course, a variety of grappa-based cocktails.

5. The Sella Ronda – The Hidden Ski Circuit

- **Location**: Dolomites, Trentino-Alto Adige region
- **Why Visit**: The **Sella Ronda** is a skiing circuit that loops around the **Sella Massif** in the Dolomites, offering skiers a chance to experience some of the most spectacular mountain landscapes in the world. Though popular among avid skiers, it's far less crowded than some of Italy's other ski resorts.
- **Highlights**:
    - **Ski Circuit**: The circuit covers 26 miles of ski slopes, connecting four ski resorts: **Corvara**, **Arabba**, **Canazei**, and **Selva di Val Gardena**.
    - **Views**: The route offers stunning panoramic views of the **Dolomites**, a UNESCO World Heritage site.
    - **Off-Slope Activities**: Non-skiers can enjoy snowshoeing, winter hiking, and cozy mountain lodges.
- **Visitor Services**:
    - Ski rental and passes are available at various locations along the circuit.
    - There are plenty of **mountain huts** serving local cuisine and hot drinks, making it a great spot for a break.

6. The Gardens of Trauttmansdorff Castle – A Hidden Botanical Paradise

- **Location**: Merano, South Tyrol
- **Why Visit**: The **Gardens of Trauttmansdorff Castle** are a stunning and expansive collection of botanical gardens, located at the foot of the **South Tyrolean Alps**. Often overlooked by tourists, this hidden gem offers lush landscapes and a tranquil escape from busy cities.
- **Highlights**:
    - **Themed Gardens**: The gardens feature more than 80 different garden landscapes from around the world, including a **Japanese Garden**, **Mediterranean Garden**, and **Water Garden**.

- ○ **Castle Museum**: Learn about the history of the area at the museum housed inside the castle, including its connection to Empress **Sisi of Austria**.
  - ○ **Panoramic Views**: The garden offers incredible views over the town of Merano and the surrounding mountains.
- **Visitor Services**:
  - ○ The **gardens** are open year-round, with different flora in bloom depending on the season.
  - ○ There are **guided tours** available to learn about the gardens' history and plant species.

7. The Fortresses of Puglia – Hidden Military Wonders

- **Location**: Puglia region
- **Why Visit**: Although Puglia is often overshadowed by other regions of Northern Italy, its **fortresses** offer a glimpse into its military past. These often-overlooked sites have historical significance and offer a quiet escape from Italy's more tourist-heavy regions.
- **Highlights**:
  - ○ **Castel del Monte**: A 13th-century castle and UNESCO World Heritage site, it's famous for its unusual octagonal shape.
  - ○ **Fortified Coastal Towers**: Along the Puglia coastline, you can find **defensive towers** used during medieval times to protect against invaders.
  - ○ **Historic Towns**: Explore the historical centers of **Andria**, **Altamura**, and **Molfetta**, which are full of charming streets and architecture.
- **Visitor Services**:
  - ○ Guided tours are available at **Castel del Monte** and some of the other fortresses.
  - ○ **Local accommodations** are available, with many being housed in historic buildings.

Northern Italy has many hidden gems waiting to be explored. From the medieval charm of **Cividale del Friuli** to the serene beauty of **Lake Orta**, these off-the-beaten-path destinations allow you to experience Italy's lesser-known treasures. Whether you're hiking in remote national parks or sipping local grappa in Bassano del Grappa, these hidden gems offer a chance to explore authentic Italian culture, history, and natural beauty without the crowds.

12.2 Day Trips from Major Cities

If you're staying in one of Northern Italy's iconic cities, such as **Milan**, **Venice**, **Florence**, or **Verona**, there are numerous amazing day trips you can take to explore the surrounding areas. Whether you're looking for a relaxing escape to a scenic lake, a historical adventure in a charming town, or a nature-filled experience in the mountains, Northern Italy offers plenty of options. Here are some of the best day trips from major cities in the region:

1. Day Trip from Milan: Lake Como

- **Location**: About 1 hour north of Milan
- **Why Visit**: **Lake Como** is famous for its breathtaking natural beauty, charming lakeside towns, and luxurious villas. A short train ride or drive from Milan brings you to one of Italy's most scenic locations.
- **Highlights**:
    - **Bellagio**: Known as the "Pearl of the Lake," this picturesque town offers cobbled streets, stunning villas, and breathtaking views over the lake.
    - **Villa Carlotta**: A beautiful villa and botanical garden in **Tremezzo**, with stunning views of the lake and surrounding mountains.
    - **Varenna**: A charming lakeside village with beautiful lakeside promenades, colorful houses, and the historic **Villa Monastero**.
    - **Boat Tour**: Take a relaxing boat tour around the lake to enjoy the scenic views and visit multiple lakeside towns.
- **Travel Tips**:
    - Trains from Milan to Como take about 1 hour, and boat rides between towns are frequent during the summer months.
    - **Visitor Services**: Many lakeside restaurants offer local cuisine, including **risotto con pesce persico** (perch fish risotto).

2. Day Trip from Venice: The Murano, Burano, and Torcello Islands

- **Location**: About 30 minutes by vaporetto (water bus) from Venice
- **Why Visit**: The **Venetian Lagoon** is home to several beautiful islands that offer a quieter, more traditional atmosphere compared to the hustle and bustle of Venice.
- **Highlights**:
    - **Murano**: Famous for its centuries-old glassmaking tradition, visit the **glass factories** and **Murano Glass Museum** to see live demonstrations and shop for authentic glass products.

- **Burano**: Known for its brightly colored houses and lace-making tradition, this picturesque island offers the perfect setting for a leisurely stroll and photography.
- **Torcello**: One of the quietest and least visited islands, it is home to **Byzantine mosaics** in the **Cathedral of Santa Maria Assunta** and a serene atmosphere.
- **Travel Tips**:
    - Vaporetto tours run regularly between the islands, and many tours offer a combination of visits to all three islands.
    - **Visitor Services**: Restaurants on Burano serve fresh seafood and traditional Venetian dishes, such as **risotto di pesce**.

3. Day Trip from Florence: Pisa and Lucca

- **Location**: About 1 hour from Florence by train
- **Why Visit**: Both **Pisa** and **Lucca** are easily accessible from Florence and offer unique experiences. Pisa is world-renowned for its Leaning Tower, while Lucca is known for its well-preserved medieval city walls and charming atmosphere.
- **Highlights**:
    - **Pisa**: Visit the **Piazza dei Miracoli** to see the famous **Leaning Tower of Pisa**, along with the **Cathedral of Pisa** and **Baptistry**.
    - **Lucca**: A medieval gem, explore the charming **city center**, walk or cycle along the **city's well-preserved Renaissance walls**, and visit the **Guinigi Tower** for panoramic views.
    - **San Michele in Foro**: A beautiful church in the heart of Lucca, showcasing stunning Romanesque architecture.
- **Travel Tips**:
    - Both cities are easily reachable by train from Florence, with Pisa taking about 1 hour and Lucca about 1.5 hours.
    - **Visitor Services**: Both cities offer plenty of cafes and local restaurants where you can try specialties like **tordelli lucchesi** (pasta) in Lucca and **cecina** (chickpea flour cake) in Pisa.

4. Day Trip from Milan: Bergamo

- **Location**: About 1 hour northeast of Milan
- **Why Visit**: **Bergamo** is an enchanting city located on a hilltop, offering stunning views, beautiful architecture, and a rich history. It is often overlooked by tourists, making it a peaceful alternative to the more crowded Milan.
- **Highlights**:

- **Città Alta (Upper Town)**: Wander through the medieval heart of Bergamo, with its cobblestone streets, **Piazza Vecchia**, and the impressive **Basilica di Santa Maria Maggiore**.
      - **Venetian Walls**: Explore the **16th-century defensive walls**, which are part of UNESCO World Heritage.
      - **Accademia Carrara**: Art lovers will appreciate this gallery, which houses works by **Raffaello**, **Botticelli**, and **Tiziano**.
  - **Travel Tips**:
      - Bergamo is easily accessible by train from Milan (about 1 hour) or by car.
      - **Visitor Services**: The city has many quaint restaurants offering local dishes like **polenta e osei** (polenta with small birds).

5. Day Trip from Milan: Cinque Terre

- **Location**: About 3 hours by train from Milan
- **Why Visit**: Although a bit further from Milan, **Cinque Terre** is a must-see for nature lovers and hikers. This UNESCO World Heritage site consists of five colorful fishing villages perched along steep cliffs overlooking the Ligurian Sea.
- **Highlights**:
    - **Monterosso al Mare**: The largest of the five villages, perfect for a relaxing day at the beach or hiking along the cliffs.
    - **Vernazza**: Known for its vibrant harbor and medieval charm, Vernazza is one of the most photogenic villages.
    - **Riomaggiore**: Explore the picturesque streets and enjoy the views from the **Lover's Lane (Via dell'Amore)**.
    - **Hiking Trails**: The **Sentiero Azzurro** connects the five villages and offers spectacular views of the coastline.
- **Travel Tips**:
    - Take a train to **La Spezia** and then connect to the Cinque Terre villages.
    - **Visitor Services**: Many local restaurants serve seafood, and there are opportunities for boat tours along the coastline.

6. Day Trip from Venice: The Euganean Hills

- **Location**: About 40 minutes southwest of Venice
- **Why Visit**: The **Euganean Hills** are a hidden gem in the Veneto region, offering lush vineyards, thermal spas, and historic towns. The area is perfect for a relaxing day trip that combines nature and history.
- **Highlights**:
    - **Monselice**: A historic town with a **medieval castle** and lovely parks. The **Castello di Monselice** is perched on the Euganean Hills, providing panoramic views of the surrounding area.

- **Abano Terme**: One of Italy's most famous spa towns, known for its thermal waters and wellness resorts.
- **Travel Tips**:
  - Travel by train to **Abano Terme** and explore the hill towns by bus or car.
  - **Visitor Services**: Several spas in Abano Terme offer relaxation treatments, and there are local eateries serving **Venetian specialties**.

These day trips from Northern Italy's major cities offer a perfect way to explore the diverse landscapes, rich history, and local culture of the region. From the lakes of **Como** and **Garda** to the historical gems of **Pisa** and **Lucca**, there's something for every traveler, whether you're interested in art, nature, history.

Chapter 13. Maps and Resources

13.1 Regional and City Maps

When traveling in Northern Italy, having access to detailed maps can significantly enhance your experience by helping you navigate the cities, regions, and scenic routes. Whether you're planning a trip around the **Italian Alps**, venturing into the historic towns of **Tuscany**, or exploring the romantic canals of **Venice**, reliable maps are essential for planning your itinerary and getting around. Below is an overview of the types of maps available and useful resources to assist in your travel planning.

1. Regional Maps of Northern Italy

- **Why You Need Them**: Regional maps provide an overview of Northern Italy's geography, allowing travelers to plan longer road trips, train journeys, and regional explorations. These maps highlight major highways, mountain ranges, lakes, and tourist hubs.

- **Key Features**:

    - **Highway and Road Networks**: Regional maps show the major motorways (autostrade) connecting cities like **Milan**, **Venice**, and **Verona** as well as the scenic routes through the **Dolomites** and **Lakes Region**.
    - **Lakes and Mountains**: Maps of **Lake Como**, **Lake Garda**, and **Lake Maggiore** are crucial for planning boat rides, hikes, and visits to surrounding towns and villages.
    - **Rail and Transport Routes**: Some regional maps include rail networks, highlighting train connections between cities and towns.
- **Where to Find Them**:

    - **Official Tourist Websites** of Northern Italy's regions often offer downloadable maps.
    - **Apps like Google Maps or Maps.me** allow for offline access to regional maps.
    - **Travel Bookstores or Tourist Information Centers**: These locations often provide physical maps for visitors.

2. City Maps for Major Destinations

- **Why You Need Them**: City maps are invaluable for navigating specific urban areas, particularly when exploring historic centers or neighborhoods with winding streets, like **Venice**, **Florence**, or **Milan**. These maps usually indicate key attractions, public transport stations, restaurants, and more.

Milan City Map

- **Key Features**:

  - **Duomo and Surroundings**: Maps of Milan's **Duomo Square** and the **Galleria Vittorio Emanuele II** help you plan visits to major landmarks.
  - **Public Transport**: Milan's metro, tram, and bus system are well-marked on city maps, making it easier to explore the city efficiently.
  - **Shopping Districts**: Find locations for Milan's high-end shopping streets, including **Via della Spiga** and **Corso Venezia**.
- **Where to Find Them**:

  - **Tourist Information Centers** in Milan (such as at the Central Station) offer detailed city maps.
  - **Milan Metro Stations**: Many metro stations provide free maps of the metro system, along with points of interest in the city.

Venice City Map

- **Key Features**:

  - **Canals and Bridges**: A map of Venice will highlight the city's famous canals, key landmarks like **Piazza San Marco**, and important bridges such as the **Rialto Bridge** and **Accademia Bridge**.
  - **Vaporetto Stops**: Venice's water bus stops are marked on most maps, offering convenient routes to key destinations like the islands of **Murano**, **Burano**, and **Torcello**.
  - **Walking Routes**: Venice maps often include walking routes to help you navigate its maze of narrow streets.
- **Where to Find Them**:

  - **Tourist Information Centers** in **Piazza San Marco** and other main squares offer free city maps.
  - **Venetian Hotels** typically provide maps to guests upon arrival.

Florence City Map

- **Key Features**:
    - **Historic Center**: Maps of Florence focus on the city's UNESCO-listed historic center, pointing out landmarks such as the **Duomo, Piazza della Signoria**, and the **Uffizi Gallery**.
    - **Walking Tours**: City maps often mark the best routes for walking tours, ideal for exploring the historic streets and squares.
    - **Public Transportation**: Maps of Florence's bus routes help navigate the city's limited public transportation system.
- **Where to Find Them**:
    - **Tourist Information Centers** around the **Santa Maria Novella Station** and **Piazza del Duomo** provide free maps.
    - **Florence Travel Websites** offer downloadable city maps and guides.

Verona City Map

- **Key Features**:
    - **Roman Landmarks**: Verona maps highlight **the Verona Arena, Casa di Giulietta** (Juliet's house), and other significant Roman sites.
    - **Historic Center**: These maps showcase the pedestrian-friendly city center and major streets like **Corso Porta Nuova**.
    - **Walking and Cycling Routes**: Some maps feature walking or cycling trails through Verona, leading visitors through scenic parts of the city.
- **Where to Find Them**:
    - **Tourist Information Centers** near **Piazza Bra** or **Verona Porta Nuova Station** offer city maps.
    - **Verona Official Website** also provides downloadable versions of city maps.

3. Specialized Maps for Specific Regions

For visitors interested in more niche aspects of Northern Italy, such as **ski resorts**, specialized maps are available to help you explore further.

Ski Resort Maps (e.g., Dolomites, Sestriere)

- **Key Features**:

    - **Ski Trails**: These maps show the various ski slopes, difficulty levels, and lift systems in ski resorts like **Cortina d'Ampezzo** or **Val Gardena**.
    - **Resort Facilities**: Maps include ski rental shops, ski schools, restaurants, and accommodations in the vicinity.
    - **Mountain Routes**: Detailed routes for snowboarding, cross-country skiing, and hiking trails in the mountains.
- **Where to Find Them**:

    - **Ski Resorts' Official Websites** often offer downloadable trail maps.
    - **Ski Pass and Resort Ticket Offices** also provide printed maps when you arrive at the resort.

4. Digital Maps and Apps

- **Google Maps**: Comprehensive coverage of Northern Italy's cities and regions, useful for walking, driving, or public transport navigation.
- **Maps.me**: Offers offline access to detailed maps of Northern Italy, making it useful for travel in remote areas.
- **Rome2Rio**: Excellent for planning your journey between cities, showing transportation options (train, bus, flight) and durations.
- **Citymapper**: Especially useful for public transport routes in cities like **Milan** and **Florence**.

Whether you prefer digital or printed resources, having access to detailed maps of **Northern Italy's regions and cities** will help you navigate the area with ease. From planning your trip through scenic landscapes and to getting around the bustling city streets of **Milan** or **Venice**, a map will enhance your travel experience and ensure you don't miss out on the hidden gems of this incredible region.

13.2 Useful Travel Apps

In today's digital age, travel apps can make navigating through Northern Italy more efficient, enjoyable, and stress-free. From mapping out routes to finding the best local restaurants and tracking transportation schedules, here are some of the most essential travel apps to have on your phone when exploring Northern Italy.

1. Google Maps

- **Description**: Google Maps is the go-to navigation app for travelers in Northern Italy. It provides real-time GPS navigation, traffic updates, walking routes, and public transport directions. Whether you're walking through **Venice**'s narrow streets or driving to a vineyard in **Langhe**, Google Maps is your reliable guide.

- **Key Features**:

    - **Real-time Traffic Updates**: Avoid delays with live traffic information.
    - **Public Transport Directions**: Plan your trips using buses, trams, and trains in cities like **Milan** and **Florence**.
    - **Offline Maps**: Download maps of specific areas and use them offline when internet connectivity is limited.
    - **Street View**: Explore landmarks and areas virtually before visiting.
- **Where to Use It**: Available worldwide for iOS and Android.

- **Website**: Google Maps

2. Citymapper

- **Description**: A powerful app for public transportation, Citymapper is especially useful in cities like **Milan**, **Venice**, and **Florence**, where navigating public transit can be complex. It integrates all forms of transport, including buses, trams, trains, and even walking routes.

- **Key Features**:

    - **Public Transport Routes**: Provides detailed, real-time public transportation schedules and alternative routes.
    - **Live Updates**: Includes live updates on delays and disruptions.
    - **Real-time ETAs**: Get accurate expected arrival times for public transit.
    - **Multimodal Routes**: Combines different transportation modes (e.g., tram + walking) for the best route.
- **Where to Use It**: Available in select cities, including **Milan**, for iOS and Android.

- **Website**: Citymapper

3. Rome2Rio

- **Description**: Rome2Rio is perfect for those planning longer trips between major cities in Northern Italy, such as **Milan** to **Verona** or **Venice** to **Florence**. The app offers multi-modal transport options, showing you how to travel by plane, train, bus, or car.

- **Key Features**:

    - **Route Suggestions**: Get suggested routes between cities or regions, including trains, flights, buses, and driving.
    - **Cost Estimates**: Estimates of travel costs for each mode of transport.
    - **Duration Estimates**: Estimated journey time for all travel options.
    - **Integrated Booking**: Allows you to book your transport directly through the app.
- **Where to Use It**: Available for iOS and Android.

- **Website**: Rome2Rio

4. TripAdvisor

- **Description**: TripAdvisor is one of the most trusted travel apps, helping you discover the best hotels, restaurants, and attractions in Northern Italy. With millions of user reviews and ratings, it provides insights into where to stay, eat, and explore.

- **Key Features**:

    - **Hotel & Restaurant Reviews**: Access thousands of reviews and ratings on accommodations, restaurants, and attractions.
    - **Activity Suggestions**: Discover things to do, whether you're in **Milan**, **Lake Como**, or **Venice**.
    - **Booking Feature**: Allows you to book hotels, tours, and restaurants directly from the app.
    - **Travel Community**: Participate in forums and ask locals or other travelers for advice.
- **Where to Use It**: Available for iOS and Android.

- **Website**: TripAdvisor

5. Yelp

- **Description**: Yelp is another great app for finding highly-rated restaurants, cafes, bars, and local businesses in Northern Italy. It's particularly useful for foodies looking to discover hidden gems away from the touristy spots.

- **Key Features**:

    - **Local Recommendations**: Browse through restaurant reviews, ratings, photos, and menus from locals and fellow travelers.
    - **User-Generated Content**: Discover insider tips and experiences from other users.
    - **Search Filters**: Filter your search based on type of cuisine, location, price, and rating.
    - **Reservation Options**: Some restaurants allow you to book a table directly through Yelp.
- **Where to Use It**: Available for iOS and Android.

- **Website**: Yelp

6. AllTrails

- **Description**: Perfect for nature lovers, **AllTrails** offers a detailed database of hiking, walking, and cycling trails across Northern Italy, including the **Dolomites**, **Lake Garda**, and **Cinque Terre**. Whether you want an easy stroll or a challenging mountain climb, this app provides valuable information on each route.

- **Key Features**:

    - **Trail Details**: Offers information on trail difficulty, length, elevation gain, and estimated time.
    - **User Reviews**: Get insights and recommendations from fellow hikers.
    - **Interactive Maps**: Detailed maps with GPS tracking to help you navigate trails.
    - **Offline Maps**: Download trails for offline use when there is no signal.
- **Where to Use It**: Available for iOS and Android.

- **Website**: AllTrails

7. The Fork

- **Description**: The Fork (also known as **LaFourchette**) is a restaurant reservation app that allows you to book tables in advance at some of the best restaurants in Northern Italy. It's perfect for securing reservations at popular spots in **Milan**, **Venice**, or **Florence**.

- **Key Features**:

    - **Restaurant Reservations**: Make reservations at top restaurants, with the ability to filter by cuisine, rating, and location.
    - **Discounts and Offers**: Occasionally, The Fork offers discounts or special deals at participating restaurants.
    - **User Reviews**: Browse reviews and recommendations before booking your table.
- **Where to Use It**: Available for iOS and Android.

- **Website**: The Fork

8. Waze

- **Description**: **Waze** is a community-driven navigation app that provides real-time traffic information, road conditions, and even speed traps. It's ideal for driving in Northern Italy, especially when traveling between cities or through mountainous terrain.

- **Key Features**:

    - **Traffic Alerts**: Get live updates on road conditions, accidents, or traffic jams.
    - **Speed Trap Warnings**: Alerts you to potential speed cameras, making it ideal for driving in unfamiliar areas.
    - **Route Optimization**: Waze helps you avoid heavy traffic by providing alternative routes based on real-time data.
- **Where to Use It**: Available for iOS and Android.

- **Website**: Waze

9. Trenitalia

- **Description**: Trenitalia is the official app for Italy's national railway system. It allows you to check schedules, book tickets, and get information about train routes, from high-speed trains to regional options, making it indispensable for traveling between cities like **Milan**, **Venice**, and **Florence**.

- **Key Features**:
    - **Train Schedules**: Check departure and arrival times for trains across Italy.
    - **Ticket Booking**: Purchase tickets and receive mobile boarding passes.
    - **Real-time Updates**: Get updates on delays or cancellations for your train.
- **Where to Use It**: Available for iOS and Android.

- **Website**: Trenitalia

10. Komoot

- **Description**: For adventure seekers, **Komoot** is an excellent app for outdoor activities like hiking, biking, and mountain biking. It features detailed routes and trail information across Northern Italy, including the **Alps** and **Dolomites**.

- **Key Features**:
    - **Route Planning**: Plan routes for hiking, biking, and mountain biking.
    - **Offline Maps**: Download routes for offline access in remote areas.
    - **Turn-by-Turn Navigation**: Provides navigation guidance for outdoor activities.
- **Where to Use It**: Available for iOS and Android.

- **Website**: Komoot

These travel apps are incredibly useful for ensuring a smooth and memorable trip to Northern Italy. Whether you're navigating through urban streets, exploring the countryside, booking tickets, or seeking local recommendations, these apps will help enhance your travel experience. Be sure to download them before your journey to make the most of your Northern Italian adventure.

13.3 Local Contacts and Websites

When traveling to Northern Italy, having access to local resources and contacts can be a game-changer, ensuring you have the support you need in case of emergencies or for planning your activities. Here's a list of essential local contacts and websites that can make your trip smoother and more enjoyable.

1. Tourist Information Centers

These centers are invaluable for getting local advice, brochures, maps, and other useful resources. You'll find them in most major cities, towns, and tourist hotspots across Northern Italy.

- **Milan Tourist Information**

  - **Location**: Milan Central Station and other major tourist spots
  - **Website**: Milan Tourist Information
  - **Phone**: +39 02 8515 6252
  - **Hours**: Monday to Saturday, 9:00 AM – 6:00 PM

- **Venice Tourist Information**

  - **Location**: Piazzale Roma and St. Mark's Square
  - **Website**: Visit Venice
  - **Phone**: +39 041 529 8711
  - **Hours**: 10:00 AM – 6:00 PM daily

- **Florence Tourist Information**

  - **Location**: Florence Central Station and Piazza del Duomo
  - **Website**: Tourism in Florence
  - **Phone**: +39 055 290 832
  - **Hours**: Monday to Saturday, 9:00 AM – 5:00 PM

2. Emergency Services

In case of emergencies, here are the essential contacts you need while traveling in Northern Italy:

- **Emergency Services (Police, Fire, Ambulance)**

  - **Phone**: 112 (EU-wide emergency number)
  - **Website**: Emergency Services Italy

- **Medical Assistance (Hospitals and Clinics)**

    - **Milan**: Ospedale Niguarda

        - **Phone**: +39 02 6444 2222
        - **Website**: [Ospedale Niguarda](#)
    - **Venice**: Ospedale Civile di Venezia

        - **Phone**: +39 041 529 8111
        - **Website**: [Ospedale Civile di Venezia](#)
    - **Florence**: Ospedale Careggi

        - **Phone**: +39 055 794 1111
        - **Website**: [Ospedale Careggi](#)

3. Public Transportation Websites

For traveling between cities and regions, public transport is a convenient option in Northern Italy. These websites provide schedules, ticket information, and more.

- **Trenitalia (National Train Service)**

    - **Website**: [Trenitalia](#)
    - **Phone**: +39 06 6847 4991 (for customer support)
- **ATAC (Public Transport in Rome and Surroundings)**

    - **Website**: [ATAC](#)
    - **Phone**: +39 06 57003 (for assistance)
- **ACTV (Venice Public Transport)**

    - **Website**: [ACTV Venice](#)
    - **Phone**: +39 041 528 9988
- **TAM (Trentino Mobilità)**

    - **Website**: [Trentino Mobilità](#)
    - **Phone**: +39 0461 210711

4. Tourist Websites for Regional Information

Each region in Northern Italy has its own tourism portal with detailed information on activities, events, accommodation, and local tips.

- **Tourism in Lombardy (Milan)**

    - **Website**: Visit Lombardy
- **Veneto Tourism (Venice and Surroundings)**

    - **Website**: Veneto Tourism
- **Tuscany Tourism (Florence and the Region)**

    - **Website**: Visit Tuscany
- **Trentino Tourism (Trentino and Dolomites)**

    - **Website**: Visit Trentino
- **Emilia-Romagna Tourism**

    - **Website**: Visit Emilia-Romagna
- **Friuli Venezia Giulia Tourism**

    - **Website**: Visit Friuli Venezia Giulia

5. Embassy and Consulate Contacts

For assistance in case of emergencies, passport loss, or other consular needs, here are the details for foreign embassies and consulates in Italy.

- **U.S. Embassy in Italy**

    - **Location**: Via Vittorio Veneto 121, 00187 Rome, Italy
    - **Phone**: +39 06 4674 1
    - **Website**: U.S. Embassy Italy
- **UK Embassy in Italy**

    - **Location**: Via XX Settembre 80a, 00187 Rome, Italy
    - **Phone**: +39 06 4220 0001
    - **Website**: UK Embassy Italy
- **Australian Embassy in Italy**

    - **Location**: Via di San Michele 9, 00153 Rome, Italy
    - **Phone**: +39 06 854 3701
    - **Website**: Australian Embassy Italy

6. Local Event and Festival Websites

For travelers interested in local events, festivals, and cultural happenings, here are some useful websites to check for the latest events in Northern Italy:

- **Milan Fashion Week**
    - **Website**: Milan Fashion Week
- **Venice Carnival**
    - **Website**: Venice Carnival
- **Florence International Arts Festival**
    - **Website**: Florence Arts Festival
- **Verona Opera Festival**
    - **Website**: Verona Opera Festival

7. Local Emergency Numbers

- **Police**: 112 (EU-wide emergency number)
- **Ambulance**: 118
- **Fire Department**: 115
- **Coast Guard (for Lakes)**: 1530

Having access to local resources, emergency numbers, and regional websites can help make your trip to Northern Italy more efficient, safe, and enjoyable. Whether you're navigating transportation, needing medical assistance, or simply looking for tourist attractions, these contacts and websites are indispensable to a successful and stress-free journey.

Chapter 14. Final Thoughts and Travel Tips

14.1 Making the Most of Your Trip

Northern Italy offers a wide array of experiences, from the bustling streets of Milan to the serene beauty of Lake Como. To truly immerse yourself in the culture, history, and natural wonders of the region, here are some final travel tips to ensure that you make the most of your visit.

1. Embrace Local Traditions and Slow Travel

One of the best ways to experience Northern Italy is to embrace its slower pace of life. Italians value quality over quantity, especially when it comes to food, coffee, and social interactions. Take time to sit down and enjoy a cappuccino in the morning or savor a leisurely lunch at a local trattoria. Don't rush through your days—immerse yourself in the culture by allowing for plenty of time to simply enjoy the moment. Slow travel is also the perfect way to explore Northern Italy's beautiful countryside, villages, and scenic lakes.

2. Plan Ahead, but Be Flexible

While Northern Italy is rich in well-known tourist attractions, there are also countless hidden gems waiting to be discovered. It's a good idea to plan your itinerary, but also leave room for spontaneous detours. Some of the best experiences happen when you take an unexpected turn down a charming alleyway or discover a quiet village off the beaten path. Be flexible with your plans and open to the surprises the region has to offer.

3. Learn a Few Basic Italian Phrases

While many Italians in major cities speak English, especially in tourist areas, learning a few basic Italian phrases can go a long way in creating connections with locals. Simple greetings like "Buongiorno" (Good morning), "Grazie" (Thank you), and "Per favore" (Please) are appreciated and can enhance your experience. Understanding the language, even at a basic level, will also help you navigate menus, signs, and daily interactions more smoothly.

4. Take Advantage of Local Public Transport

Northern Italy has an excellent public transport system, which can be both affordable and convenient for getting around. Trains and buses connect all major cities, and many smaller towns can be easily reached by public transport. In cities like Milan, Venice, and Florence, walking or using trams and metro systems can save you time and allow you to see more of the area. Renting a bike or using regional train services also makes it easy to explore the countryside, lakes, and mountains at your own pace.

5. Stay Hydrated and Protect Yourself from the Sun

Northern Italy enjoys a Mediterranean climate, which means that summers can get hot and dry, particularly in cities like Milan and Florence. Always carry a water bottle with you, and be sure to drink plenty of water, especially when sightseeing. Wearing sunscreen, sunglasses, and a hat can help protect you from the sun, particularly when exploring outdoor attractions or hiking in the Italian Alps or the Dolomites.

6. Prioritize Cultural Sensitivity

Italians take great pride in their cultural heritage and traditions. To make the most of your trip, it's important to be mindful of local customs and practices. Dress modestly when visiting churches and religious sites, and always respect the local environment. Keep noise levels low when in public places, especially during meals, as Italians place great value on quiet, respectful social interactions. Always greet people politely with "Buongiorno" in the morning or "Buona sera" in the evening, and take the time to say "Arrivederci" (Goodbye) when leaving a place.

7. Take Time to Explore the Surrounding Areas

While Northern Italy's major cities are certainly worth visiting, don't overlook the surrounding regions. Explore the rolling vineyards of the Langhe in Piedmont, the quaint medieval villages of Umbria, or the charming lakeside towns near Lake Garda. These regions offer a more relaxed, authentic Italian experience, with opportunities to visit local ries, historic sites, and hidden gems that you may not find in the larger cities.

8. Avoid Overpacking

Northern Italy offers a diverse range of activities, from strolling through cities and towns to hiking in the Alps or boating on the lakes. To fully enjoy your experience, avoid overpacking. Pack light and versatile clothing that can transition between different activities. Comfortable walking shoes are essential for exploring cities, while outdoor gear is necessary if you plan on hiking or skiing. Always check the weather forecast before your trip and adjust your packing accordingly.

9. Respect Nature and Environment

Many parts of Northern Italy, including the Italian Alps and the lakes region, are known for their stunning natural beauty. Be sure to respect the environment by sticking to marked trails when hiking, avoiding littering, and supporting eco-friendly businesses. If you're visiting the Dolomites or other natural parks, make sure to follow Leave No Trace principles, preserving the landscape for future generations.

Northern Italy is a treasure trove of diverse landscapes, rich history, and mouthwatering cuisine. Whether you're drawn to its sophisticated cities, serene lakes, charming villages, or majestic mountains, there is something for every traveler to enjoy. By taking the time to plan ahead, embracing local traditions, and staying open to new experiences, you can create unforgettable memories and truly immerse yourself in the beauty of Northern Italy.

14.2 FAQs for First-Time Visitors

Traveling to Northern Italy for the first time can be an exciting yet daunting experience, especially with so much to see and do. To help you navigate your journey, here are some frequently asked questions (FAQs) that will provide you with useful insights and tips for making the most of your visit.

1. What is the best time to visit Northern Italy?

The best time to visit Northern Italy depends on your preferences:

- **Spring (April to June)**: Ideal for pleasant weather, fewer crowds, and the beauty of blooming flowers and landscapes.
- **Summer (July to August)**: Perfect for enjoying lakes and mountains, expect larger crowds and higher prices, especially in tourist-heavy areas.
- **Autumn (September to October)**: A great time for enthusiasts regions, including Piedmont and Tuscany, hold grape harvest fe weather is still warm but more comfortable.
- **Winter (December to March)**: A fantastic time for skiing i and the Alps, with winter sports lovers flocking to the region.

2. Do I need to speak Italian to visit Northern Italy?

While it's not essential to speak Italian, learning a few (Good morning), "Grazie" (Thank you), and "Per fav your experience. In major tourist areas like Milan speak English, but outside of these areas, English

3. How can I get around Northern Italy

Northern Italy has an excellent transportation system, with various options depending on where you're traveling:

- **Train**: Trains are the most efficient way to travel between major cities like Milan, Venice, and Florence. The Trenitalia and Italo train services are fast and reliable.
- **Public Transport**: In cities like Milan, Venice, and Florence, trams, buses, and metros are the best ways to get around. Many cities offer day passes for tourists.
- **Car Rental**: Renting a car is a good option if you plan to visit smaller towns or explore the countryside. However, be aware of ZTL zones (limited traffic zones) in many cities.
- **Bicycles and Boats**: In places like Milan and Venice, you can rent bicycles or take boat rides (like the Vaporetto in Venice) to explore at a leisurely pace.

4. What is the dress code in Northern Italy?

Italians are known for their fashion sense, and while you don't need to dress as fashion-forward as the locals, it's a good idea to dress neatly and stylishly, especially in major cities. When visiting religious sites, such as churches or cathedrals, it's recommended to dress modestly. This means covering your shoulders and avoiding shorts in some places. Comfortable walking shoes are essential for sightseeing.

5. Are credit cards widely accepted in Northern Italy?

Yes, credit cards are widely accepted in Northern Italy, especially in larger cities and tourist destinations. However, it's always a good idea to carry some cash for smaller purchases, especially in rural areas, markets, or smaller shops. ATMs are easy to find, and most accept international cards. The official currency is the Euro (€).

Tipping customary in Northern Italy?

Tipping is appreciated but not mandatory in Northern Italy. In restaurants, a service charge (usually around 10-15%) is often included in the bill, so additional tips are not expected. However, if you receive exceptional service, leaving a small tip (5-10%) is a nice gesture. For taxis and hotel porters, rounding up the fare or leaving a couple of euros is common.

Some must-see attractions in Northern Italy?

Top attractions include:

- Duomo Cathedral, Leonardo da Vinci's "The Last Supper," and the fashion district.
- St. Mark's Square, the Grand Canal, and the Rialto Bridge.

- **Florence**: The Uffizi Gallery, Florence Cathedral (Duomo), and Ponte Vecchio.
- **Lake Como**: The stunning lakeside views, Bellagio, and luxurious villas.
- **The Dolomites**: Ski resorts, hiking trails, and charming alpine villages.

8. Is Northern Italy safe for travelers?

Northern Italy is generally considered very safe for tourists. However, like in any major tourist destination, it's essential to stay vigilant and take basic precautions. Watch out for pickpockets, especially in crowded areas like train stations and tourist hotspots. Keep your belongings secure and avoid leaving valuables unattended.

9. What is the food like in Northern Italy?

Northern Italian cuisine is diverse and varies by region, but it's known for its rich flavors and high-quality ingredients. Common dishes include:

- **Risotto**: Particularly popular in Milan (Risotto alla Milanese).
- **Polenta**: A traditional dish often served with meats or cheese.
- **Osso Buco**: Braised veal shanks, typically served with risotto.
- **Fresh pasta**: Such as tortellini in Bologna and pappardelle in Tuscany. The region is also famous for its s, including Barolo (Piedmont), Amarone (Veneto), and Pinot Grigio (Friuli Venezia Giulia).

10. How can I stay connected while traveling in Northern Italy?

Most cities and tourist areas offer free Wi-Fi in cafes, hotels, and public spaces. If you need reliable internet access during your travels, consider purchasing a local SIM card for your phone or a portable Wi-Fi hotspot. This can be particularly useful when exploring rural areas or remote parts of Northern Italy where public Wi-Fi might be scarce.

Northern Italy is an incredible destination with something to offer every traveler, from world-class art and history to stunning landscapes and delicious cuisine. By preparing well, respecting local customs, and staying flexible with your plans, you're sure to have a memorable experience.